CIMA PUBLISHING

The Complete November 2004 CIMA Examinations Question Papers with Examiner's Answers

Final Level

ELSEVIER

AMSTERDAM BOSTON HEIDELBERG LONDON NEW YORK OXFORD
PARIS SAN DIEGO SAN FRANCISCO SINGAPORE SYDNEY TOKYO

CIMA Publishing
An imprint of Elsevier
Linacre House, Jordan Hill, Oxford OX2 8DP
30 Corporate Drive, Burlington, MA 01803

First Published 2005.

British Library Cataloguing in Publication Data
A catalogue record for this book is available from the British Library

ISBN 0 750667451

For information on all CIMA publications
visit our website at www.cimapublishing.com

Printed and bound by Antony Rowe Ltd, Eastbourne

NOVEMBER 2004 FINAL LEVEL

This book contains the **complete November 2004** CIMA Examination **Question Papers** with the **Examiner's Answers** for the **Final level**, direct from CIMA and brought to you by CIMA Publishing, an imprint of Elsevier:

Paper 12	Management Accounting Business Strategy
Paper 13	Management Accounting Financial Strategy
Paper 14	Management Accounting Information Strategy
Paper 15	Management Accounting Case Study

Also available:

A companion book containing the complete November 2004 Question papers with Examiner's Answers for the Intermediate Level. ISBN: 0750667443
Available from: www.cimapublishing.com

For all your future CIMA Qualification study needs: Official CIMA Study Systems, Revision Cards, Exam Practice Kits, and CIMA interactive CD ROMS for the new syllabus visit:

www.cimapublishing.com or complete the order form at the back of this book

CIMA

November 2004 Examinations

Final Level

Management Accounting – Business Strategy

(FLBS – Paper 12)

The answers published here have been written by the Examiner and should provide a helpful guide for both lecturers and students.

Published separately on the CIMA website (www.cimaglobal.com/students) from the end of March 2005 is a Post Examination Guide for this paper, which provides much valuable and complementary material including indicative mark information.

CIMA

Final Level

Management Accounting – Business Strategy

12

FLBS

23 November 2004

Tuesday morning

INSTRUCTIONS TO CANDIDATES

Read this page before you look at the questions

You are allowed three hours to answer this question paper.
Answer the ONE question in Section A. Answer TWO questions ONLY from Section B.
Maths Tables and Formulae are provided.

SECTION A – 50 MARKS

ANSWER THIS QUESTION

Question One

Background

The P Group is listed and is a manufacturer of sheet metal which it supplies to building contractors and vehicle manufacturers around the world. It has manufacturing operations in 25 countries, employing over 3,000 people in total.

The Chairman of the P Group believes that its exposure to unsystematic financial and economic risk is reduced by diversification of sales through world markets. The company has become leader in several of its markets and is regarded as a major multinational company.

Latest financial information for the Group

The following extracts are taken from the most recent set of published accounts:

Group Profit and Loss Statement for the year ended 30 September 2003

	$m
Group turnover	320
Group profit on ordinary activities before tax	19
Earnings per share	$0·006
Dividend per share	$0·005

P's market capitalisation is $110 million.

Manufacturing operations in Bigland

One of P Group's subsidiary manufacturing units (PB) is in a factory within the country of Bigland. It manufactures three sheet metal products, M1, M2 and M3 and sells these exclusively within Bigland. The market position of M1 is that a competitor is the market leader, whereas PB is itself the market leader in respect of its product M2. There is no clear market leader for product M3. The products are independent and do not complement each other. Performance data for each of products M1, M2 and M3 are given below for the two years ended September 2004 (the heading PB indicates the PB Company). For comparison purposes, performance data for the nearest competitor for each product is also given (the heading C indicates the nearest competitor).

	PRODUCT					
	M1		M2		M3	
	PB	*C*	*PB*	*C*	*PB*	*C*
	$m	*$m*	*$m*	*$m*	*$m*	*$m*
Year to 30 September 2003						
Turnover	6·00	16·00	4·50	1·50	2·80	2·50
Operating costs	5·40	11·00	3·20	1·00	2·10	2·20
Pre-tax operating profit	0·60	5·00	1·30	0·50	0·70	0·30
Year to 30 September 2004						
Turnover	5·80	18·00	6·40	2·40	3·70	3·40
Operating costs	5·60	12·10	4·20	1·40	2·90	3·00
Pre-tax operating profit	0·20	5·90	2·20	1·00	0·80	0·40

Management of PB is very traditional and may be regarded as classical in style. It follows the principle that the company may be engineered to work perfectly. There is clear segregation of tasks and role specialisation in place. Management is exercised through a "top down" approach with staff being largely regarded as inputs into the system motivated purely by their level of earnings. In recent years, there has been increasing staff turnover at PB which has led to an increase in costs, particularly in the areas of recruitment and training. Higher than average salaries and wages have been paid to attract staff.

Strategic review of PB

Senior management of the P Group have been concerned for a few years about the overall level of market share and profitability of PB, but other than seeking an explanation regarding the unsatisfactory performance from the Managing Director, they have taken no action. The Chairman of P Group has now decided that immediate action should be taken and has proposed four alternative options.

Each of these options is set out below. The financial consequences of each option for the next financial year are also detailed:

Option		*Financial consequences*
(i)	Withdraw from the market	Impact of closure on other P Group sales in the region (due to reduction in demand for complementary products) would reduce pre tax operating profit by $4m and the incremental cost of the closure of PB would result in a once and for all before tax cost of $2m.
(ii)	Maintain PB	Turnover of products M2 and M3 will increase by 25% each, but M1 will continue its current rate of decline. Costs for products M2 and M3 would remain in the same proportion to sales as they were for the year ended 30 September 2004. The costs for product M1 would rise to $5·8m.
(iii)	Export to Bigland	An incremental cost of the closure of PB will be a single before tax cost of $2m. Turnover for products M2 and M3 will increase by 25% each, but M1 will continue its current rate of decline. The operating costs of production will be on average 5% higher than those incurred in Bigland and transport costs will be $1m per annum to carry the products to customers in Bigland.
(iv)	Licence the products	The licence fee income will be $2m altogether for all three products. Costs of ensuring quality of production will be $0·5m and the incremental cost of the closure of PB will be a single before tax cost of $2m.

The Group Managing Director now requires a review of the impact each of the four options will have on the profitability of the group as a whole in the next financial year. At this stage, he does not require an analysis which extends beyond one year, nor does he want to consider the effects on taxation or transfer pricing just yet, as he requires a speedy review to enable him to discuss the position with the Chairman very quickly.

Required:

(a) Produce a critical appraisal of the use of the Boston Consulting Group Growth Share Matrix for the purposes of evaluating PB's product portfolio.

(10 marks)

(b) Evaluate the performance of PB for the two years ended 30 September 2003 and 2004 making any comparisons you consider appropriate with the company's competitors.

(15 marks)

(c) Evaluate the financial impact of each of the four options set out by the Chairman. Recommend, with reasons, to the P Group Managing Director which option you consider to be the most appropriate ignoring the effects of discounted cash flow, inflation, taxation and the effect of exchange rate variation.

(15 marks)

(d) Discuss the effects each of the options may have on the organisational management and structure of PB and on the group as a whole.

(10 marks)

(Total = 50 marks)

End of Section A

SECTION B – 50 MARKS

ANSWER TWO QUESTIONS ONLY

Question Two

There are several different methods of strategy formulation. Most strategists would argue, for instance, that public sector organisations mainly favour a logical, rational approach.

The senior partners of the world famous private sector management consultancy firm SPK are presently considering both the issue of their own strategy formulation and making some changes to direction of the company. SPK only deals with traditional "blue chip" companies. SPK is renowned for networking and has access to key decision makers through the personal contacts of its partners and senior managers. These contacts are felt to be at the heart of its business success. SPK places a lot of trust in the decisions made by its relatively small core of partners and senior managers who foster close relationships with clients and identify consultancy opportunities. These individuals draw together and then lead teams of (normally) freelance consultants and academics to fulfil their consultancy briefs.

Partners and senior managers are judged on the client profile and profitability levels within their personal portfolios. Individually, they are highly skilled but tend to have definite fixed opinions and to be strong willed. In addition, they work independently when deciding which business areas to target and the nature of work undertaken.

Required:

(a) Discuss the main approaches to strategy formulation and recommend the most appropriate for SPK.

(15 marks)

(b) Analyse the reasons for public sector organisations generally adopting a logical rational approach to strategy formulation and suggest how, in the absence of profitability, they can measure performance.

(10 marks)

(Total = 25 marks)

Question Three

Parachute Fund Management (PFM) has been responsible for the investment of pension and life insurance funds for the past twenty years. It claims to be a "fund manager with a difference" by seeking to gain active involvement in under-performing or poorly managed businesses. PFM requires that companies it has invested in be run in the long-term interests of the shareholders. PFM assesses such companies in terms of communication, financial, strategic and ethical performance against certain principles it has developed. (For instance, one financial principle is that "companies should have performance evaluation and incentive systems to provide managers with an incentive to deliver long term shareholder value").

PFM's belief is that there is a lack of "real" accountability between boards of directors and shareholders and that too often shareholders concentrate on short-term financial gains. PFM argues that if other investors believe that a company is poorly run they merely sell their shares and invest elsewhere. Thus boards of directors are not held properly to account over poor performance. Where it believes companies it invests in are under-performing, PFM enters into dialogue with the board and seeks changes in practice. PFM is increasingly being recognised as a major driver of change in corporate life.

Required:

(a) Evaluate the stakeholder role performed by PFM including the source of its power and apparent interest.

(13 marks)

(b) Advise an under-performing company how it should put in place appropriate performance evaluation and incentive systems to provide managers with the motivation to deliver long term shareholder value.

(12 marks)

(Total = 25 marks)

Question Four

Glaspac is a manufacturer and installer of replacement plastic windows. Glaspac prides itself on its added security features. While there are some national competitors, most are regional and recently two of Glaspac's competitors have merged. Glaspac operates in a national market and has agents who display products and distribute promotional literature in some shopping malls and large stores throughout the country. These agents collect details of potential customers for sales executives to follow up and give detailed quotations. At a planning meeting two years ago, Glaspac agreed that it could realistically achieve a turnover of $400,000 per quarter within three years. At present, it only achieves a turnover of $300,000 per quarter; a fall of $50,000 from two years ago.

Required:

(a) Analyse, by reference to gap analysis, Glaspac's position and the available options implied by the technique.

(12 marks)

(b) Discuss the relationship between gap analysis and scenario planning in the strategic process. Making reference to Glaspac, advise how these techniques might be used together.

(13 marks)

(Total = 25 marks)

Question Five

For an organisation to successfully achieve its strategies it will need to give adequate consideration to both structure and support systems. Similarly, it should consider the issue of relationship management, as all organisations are reliant on relationships with others. In varying degrees, organisations explore their boundaries of responsibility with others and many have taken the decision to outsource activities, some to the extent that they operate as "networked organisations".

The term "virtual organisations" has been used to describe an extreme form of networked organisation that has minimal owned resources and activities. Here the emphasis is almost solely upon partnership and collaboration rather than permanent staff, physical sites and formal structures. Critics feel that such organisations are unable to operate beyond the short term, citing as evidence the number of so-called "dot com" companies that have gone out of business.

Required:

(a) Discuss the key strategic issues that will lead to potential strategic strengths or weaknesses for a virtual networked organisation.

(12 marks)

(b) Discuss the benefits and difficulties of conducting an environmental analysis in an organisation that is highly networked.

(13 marks)

(Total = 25 marks)

End of paper

Maths Tables and Formulae follow

MATHS TABLES AND FORMULAE

TABLES

Present value table

Present value of $1, that is $(1+r)^{-n}$ where r = interest rate; n = number of periods until payment or receipt.

Periods	Interest rates (r)									
(n)	1%	2%	3%	4%	5%	6%	7%	8%	9%	10%
1	0.990	0.980	0.971	0.962	0.952	0.943	0.935	0.926	0.917	0.909
2	0.980	0.961	0.943	0.925	0.907	0.890	0.873	0.857	0.842	0.826
3	0.971	0.942	0.915	0.889	0.864	0.840	0.816	0.794	0.772	0.751
4	0.961	0.924	0.888	0.855	0.823	0.792	0.763	0.735	0.708	0.683
5	0.951	0.906	0.863	0.822	0.784	0.747	0.713	0.681	0.650	0.621
6	0.942	0.888	0.837	0.790	0.746	0705	0.666	0.630	0.596	0.564
7	0.933	0.871	0.813	0.760	0.711	0.665	0.623	0.583	0.547	0.513
8	0.923	0.853	0.789	0.731	0.677	0.627	0.582	0.540	0.502	0.467
9	0.914	0.837	0.766	0.703	0.645	0.592	0.544	0.500	0.460	0.424
10	0.905	0.820	0.744	0.676	0.614	0.558	0.508	0.463	0.422	0.386
11	0.896	0.804	0.722	0.650	0.585	0.527	0.475	0.429	0.388	0.350
12	0.887	0.788	0.701	0.625	0.557	0.497	0.444	0.397	0.356	0.319
13	0.879	0.773	0.681	0.601	0.530	0.469	0.415	0.368	0.326	0.290
14	0.870	0.758	0.661	0.577	0.505	0.442	0.388	0.340	0.299	0.263
15	0.861	0.743	0.642	0.555	0.481	0.417	0.362	0.315	0.275	0.239
16	0.853	0.728	0.623	0.534	0.458	0.394	0.339	0.292	0.252	0.218
17	0.844	0.714	0.605	0.513	0.436	0.371	0.317	0.270	0.231	0.198
18	0.836	0.700	0.587	0.494	0.416	0.350	0.296	0.250	0.212	0.180
19	0.828	0.686	0.570	0.475	0.396	0.331	0.277	0.232	0.194	0.164
20	0.820	0.673	0.554	0.456	0.377	0.312	0.258	0.215	0.178	0.149

Periods	Interest rates (r)									
(n)	11%	12%	13%	14%	15%	16%	17%	18%	19%	20%
1	0.901	0.893	0.885	0.877	0.870	0.862	0.855	0.847	0.840	0.833
2	0.812	0.797	0.783	0.769	0.756	0.743	0.731	0.718	0.706	0.694
3	0.731	0.712	0.693	0.675	0.658	0.641	0.624	0.609	0.593	0.579
4	0.659	0.636	0.613	0.592	0.572	0.552	0.534	0.516	0.499	0.482
5	0.593	0.567	0.543	0.519	0.497	0.476	0.456	0.437	0.419	0.402
6	0.535	0.507	0.480	0.456	0.432	0.410	0.390	0.370	0.352	0.335
7	0.482	0.452	0.425	0.400	0.376	0.354	0.333	0.314	0.296	0.279
8	0.434	0.404	0.376	0.351	0.327	0.305	0.285	0.266	0.249	0.233
9	0.391	0.361	0.333	0.308	0.284	0.263	0.243	0.225	0.209	0.194
10	0.352	0.322	0.295	0.270	0.247	0.227	0.208	0.191	0.176	0.162
11	0.317	0.287	0.261	0.237	0.215	0.195	0.178	0.162	0.148	0.135
12	0.286	0.257	0.231	0.208	0.187	0.168	0.152	0.137	0.124	0.112
13	0.258	0.229	0.204	0.182	0.163	0.145	0.130	0.116	0.104	0.093
14	0.232	0.205	0.181	0.160	0.141	0.125	0.111	0.099	0.088	0.078
15	0.209	0.183	0.160	0.140	0.123	0.108	0.095	0.084	0.079	0.065
16	0.188	0.163	0.141	0.123	0.107	0.093	0.081	0.071	0.062	0.054
17	0.170	0.146	0.125	0.108	0.093	0.080	0.069	0.060	0.052	0.045
18	0.153	0.130	0.111	0.095	0.081	0.069	0.059	0.051	0.044	0.038
19	0.138	0.116	0.098	0.083	0.070	0.060	0.051	0.043	0.037	0.031
20	0.124	0.104	0.087	0.073	0.061	0.051	0.043	0.037	0.031	0.026

Cumulative present value of $1 per annum, Receivable or Payable at the end of each year for *n* years $\frac{1-(1+r)^{-n}}{r}$

Periods	Interest rates (*r*)									
(*n*)	1%	2%	3%	4%	5%	6%	7%	8%	9%	10%
1	0.990	0.980	0.971	0.962	0.952	0.943	0.935	0.926	0.917	0.909
2	1.970	1.942	1.913	1.886	1.859	1.833	1.808	1.783	1.759	1.736
3	2.941	2.884	2.829	2.775	2.723	2.673	2.624	2.577	2.531	2.487
4	3.092	3.808	3.717	3.630	3.546	3.465	3.387	3.312	3.240	3.170
5	4.853	4.713	4.580	4.452	4.329	4.212	4.100	3.993	3.890	3.791
6	5.795	5.601	5.417	5.242	5.076	4.917	4.767	4.623	4.486	4.355
7	6.728	6.472	6.230	6.002	5.786	5.582	5.389	5.206	5.033	4.868
8	7.652	7.325	7.020	6.733	6.463	6.210	5.971	5.747	5.535	5.335
9	8.566	8.162	7.786	7.435	7.108	6.802	6.515	6.247	5.995	5.759
10	9.471	8.983	8.530	8.111	7.722	7.360	7.024	6.710	6.418	6.145
11	10.368	9.787	9.253	8.760	8.306	7.887	7.499	7.139	6.805	6.495
12	11.255	10.575	9.954	9.385	8.863	8.384	7.943	7.536	7.161	6.814
13	12.134	11.348	10.635	9.986	9.394	8.853	8.358	7.904	7.487	7.103
14	13.004	12.106	11.296	10.563	9.899	9.295	8.745	8.244	7.786	7.367
15	13.865	12.849	11.938	11.118	10.380	9.712	9.108	8.559	8.061	7.606
16	14.718	13.578	12.561	11.652	10.838	10.106	9.447	8.851	8.313	7.824
17	15.562	14.292	13.166	12.166	11.274	10.477	9.763	9.122	8.544	8.022
18	16.398	14.992	13.754	12.659	11.690	10.828	10.059	9.372	8.756	8.201
19	17.226	15.679	14.324	13.134	12.085	11.158	10.336	9.604	8.950	8.365
20	18.046	16.351	14.878	13.590	12.462	11.470	10.594	9.818	9.129	8.514

Periods	Interest rates (*r*)									
(*n*)	11%	12%	13%	14%	15%	16%	17%	18%	19%	20%
1	0.901	0.893	0.885	0.877	0.870	0.862	0.855	0.847	0.840	0.833
2	1.713	1.690	1.668	1.647	1.626	1.605	1.585	1.566	1.547	1.528
3	2.444	2.402	2.361	2.322	2.283	2.246	2.210	2.174	2.140	2.106
4	3.102	3.037	2.974	2.914	2.855	2.798	2.743	2.690	2.639	2.589
5	3.696	3.605	3.517	3.433	3.352	3.274	3.199	3.127	3.058	2.991
6	4.231	4.111	3.998	3.889	3.784	3.685	3.589	3.498	3.410	3.326
7	4.712	4.564	4.423	4.288	4.160	4.039	3.922	3.812	3.706	3.605
8	5.146	4.968	4.799	4.639	4.487	4.344	4.207	4.078	3.954	3.837
9	5.537	5.328	5.132	4.946	4.772	4.607	4.451	4.303	4.163	4.031
10	5.889	5.650	5.426	5.216	5.019	4.833	4.659	4.494	4.339	4.192
11	6.207	5.938	5.687	5.453	5.234	5.029	4.836	4.656	4.486	4.327
12	6.492	6.194	5.918	5.660	5.421	5.197	4.988	7.793	4.611	4.439
13	6.750	6.424	6.122	5.842	5.583	5.342	5.118	4.910	4.715	4.533
14	6.982	6.628	6.302	6.002	5.724	5.468	5.229	5.008	4.802	4.611
15	7.191	6.811	6.462	6.142	5.847	5.575	5.324	5.092	4.876	4.675
16	7.379	6.974	6.604	6.265	5.954	5.668	5.405	5.162	4.938	4.730
17	7.549	7.120	6.729	6.373	6.047	5.749	5.475	5.222	4.990	4.775
18	7.702	7.250	6.840	6.467	6.128	5.818	5.534	5.273	5.033	4.812
19	7.839	7.366	6.938	6.550	6.198	5.877	5.584	5.316	5.070	4.843
20	7.963	7.469	7.025	6.623	6.259	5.929	5.628	5.353	5.101	4.870

FORMULAE

Annuity

Present value of an annuity of $1 per annum, receivable or payable for *n* years, commencing in one year, discounted at *r*% per annum:

$$PV = \frac{1}{r}\left[1 - \frac{1}{[1+r]^n}\right]$$

Perpetuity

Present value of $1 per annum, payable or receivable in perpetuity, commencing in one year, discounted at *r*% per annum:

$$PV = \frac{1}{r}$$

Growing perpetuity

Present value of $1 per annum, receivable or payable, commencing in one year, growing in perpetuity at a constant rate of *g*% per annum, discounted at *r*% per annum:

$$PV = \frac{1}{r-g}$$

$$\textbf{Equivalent annual cost} = \frac{\text{PV of costs over } n \text{ years}}{n \text{ year annuity factor}}$$

The Examiner for FLBS offers to future candidates and to lecturers using this booklet for study purposes, the following background and guidance on the questions included in this examination paper.

Section A – compulsory

Question One part (a) tests candidates' ability to apply a well understood model in the particular circumstances applied in the scenario. It also allows critical thought to be demonstrated. This part of the question addresses syllabus aim 2 and to a lesser extent syllabus aim 1. Part (b) reviews the performance of the division and measures its competitiveness. In addition, this part of the question enables consideration of how vulnerable the division is to increased competitiveness. It addresses syllabus aim 5 and to a lesser extent syllabus aim 3. Part (c): Management accounting activity of reviewing strategic options within a limited time frame allowing due consideration and advice to be given to senior management of the organisation. This part addresses syllabus aims 3 and 4. Part (d) asks candidates to review the options from a different perspective other than financial and recognises the impact of strategic options on operational management resulting in the need for organisational change. This part addresses syllabus aim 4 and to a lesser extent syllabus aim 2.

Section B – two questions from four

Question Two part (a) tests the application of (probably) three well rehearsed approaches to the scenario. It also allows critical thought to be demonstrated. Part (b) tests candidates' understanding of the distinctive features of the public sector within the context of strategic approaches and performance management. It too allows critical thought to be demonstrated. This question addresses the learning outcome *"Evaluate different approaches to strategy formulation and recommend the most appropriate"* from syllabus section (i) – *Setting Objectives.*

Question Three part (a) tests candidates' understanding of shareholder and stakeholder rights, interests, power and potential influence on listed companies. This part addresses the learning outcome *"Explain the role and activities of pressure groups"* from syllabus section (ii) – *Appraising the Environment.* Part (b) tests recognition of the differing interests of shareholder groups and individuals. This part addresses the learning outcome *"Evaluate and produce a comprehensive review of performance, resources and capabilities"* from syllabus section (iii) – *Position Appraisal and Analysis.* Part (c) tests understanding of how to "incentivise" managers to achieve longer-term aspirations of a listed company. This part addresses the learning outcome *"Evaluate and produce multidimensional models of performance management"* from syllabus section (iv) – *Implementing and controlling plans.*

Question Four part (a) tests the potential to apply a meaningful framework to a realistic scenario and the strategic options arising from such an analysis. This part addresses the learning outcome *"Identify and evaluate an organisation's planning gap"* from syllabus section (iv) – *Evaluating strategic options.* Part (b) tests the relationship between two techniques and their relationship to the scenario. It too allows critical thought to be demonstrated. This part addresses the learning outcome *"Prepare and evaluate strategic scenario plans"* again from syllabus section (iv).

Question Five part (a) tests, in general terms, candidates' understanding of a distinct organisational form and the key features arising that form part of a strategic plan. This part addresses the learning outcome *"Identify the position of organisational boundaries"* from syllabus section (iii) – *Position Appraisal and Analysis.* Part (b) examines trends in contemporary organisational forms and the potential impact on the management accounting function. This part addresses the same learning outcome as part (a). Part (c) examines another dimension of networked organisations (appraising the environment) and encourages realistic speculation as to the distinctive issues this might raise. It also allows critical thought to be demonstrated. This part addresses the learning outcome *"Evaluate the availability and quality of data for environmental analysis "* from syllabus section (ii) – *Appraising the Environment.*

CIMA

The Examiners' Answers for Management Accounting – Business Strategy

SECTION A

Answer to Question One

Requirement (a)

Any business unit may provide a number of different products for its customers. In the scenario, PB Company (PB) provides only three products M1, M2 and M3. Probably the most well known model of portfolio analysis is the Boston Consulting Group (BCG) Growth Share Matrix. The model enables a business unit of a company to plot its products on a two dimensional matrix according to their rate of market growth and share of the market relative to their largest competitor.

The scenario gives insufficient information, in particular in respect of market growth, for a full analysis of the products to determine where they would be placed on the Matrix. However, an approximation can be made of where they might be placed. Given that the largest competitor for M1, the market leader, holds over three times the market share in terms of turnover, it may be considered that this product is a "question mark" but could become a "dog". On the other hand, product M2 is market leader with considerable growth between 2003 and 2004 leading to the view that it is a "cash cow". M3 is indeterminate, with many competing products in the market and therefore although PB may be the market leader (marginally) it seems that it is what the BCG matrix would regard as a "question mark".

The BCG argues that high relative market share is crucial to improve competitiveness due to the enjoyment of increased economies of scale as a result of benefits accruing from the experience curve effect. The theory is that low costs lead to increased competitiveness as the less efficient firms are driven out of the market which, in turn, results in those that remain having higher market shares. However, this analysis is based on the assumption that the experience curve effects actually take place. This, however, does not apply in all industries. Some may experience a higher cumulative volume as a result of lower unit costs if the lower unit costs themselves enable more customers to buy the product in the first place. Examples of this can be seen in the automobile industry and wine consumption. However, it is likely that the sheet metal industry will enjoy the benefits of the experience curve effects as there is likely to be a limited amount of total demand for the product and, therefore, PB will be competing for market share in a more or less static market. The exception to this is where an increase in the volume of the final product, such as automobiles, results in an increase in demand for the raw material, sheet metal.

Pricing at a level which ensures high market share may result in initial capital costs being regarded as sunk. These costs may never be recovered rendering the firm unable to provide funds for replacing capital equipment in the future if it continues to price below average total costs.

The definition of the market is also problematic. In PB's case the market may be relatively easily defined as its customer base is likely to be narrow and unfragmented. Nevertheless, is PB in the construction industry, automobile, aircraft, shipbuilding or other market? Is PB competing with companies that supply substitute products for sheet metal such as plastic?

A further complication is that the axes themselves have been criticised for being too simple in concept. Relative market share may be dependent on various factors which the matrix does not take into account. How much of PB's market share depends on its brand image and reputation or product quality or delivery lead times? The axis itself does not differentiate between factors which contribute to relative market share.

Industry growth rate is regarded as demonstrating industry attractiveness. High growth and heavy industries require considerable capital investment which means that firms which do not have such resources would not be able to compete irrespective of how attractive the industry actually is. Thus much potential competition to PB may be stifled due to the high entry barriers.

The matrix concentrates on cash flow emanating from products and assumes that the cash cows enable investment in question mark and star products turning them into cash cows themselves. The matrix makes no allowance for potential complementary products or the sharing of joint costs. In PB's case it is clear that at least some fixed costs are shared between each of the products. If M1, the "dog" product is closed down, will this adversely affect profitability of M2 and M3 because of the same level of fixed costs being spread across a smaller number of products?

Requirement (b)

Performance evaluation of PB

	M1		**M2**		**M3**	
	PB	**C**	**PB**	**C**	**PB**	**C**
	%	%	%	%	%	%
Op. Profit to Turnover (2003)	10	31	29	33	25	12
Op. Profit to Turnover (2004)	3	33	34	42	22	12
Increase (Decrease) in turnover (2003-04)	(3)	12	42	60	32	36
Increase (Decrease) in op. costs (2003-04)	4	10	31	40	38	36
Increase (Decrease) in pre tax profit (2003-04)	(66)	18	69	100	14	33

Examiner's note:
Credit also given for other relevant ratios calculated.

M1: This is a "question mark" product with severely reducing profitability due to reduction in turnover and increasing operating costs. It could easily become a "dog" product. The competitor who is market leader seems to be gaining from PB's inefficiency in producing this product with an increase in turnover of 12% offset, however, by an increase in operating costs. M1 is clearly a drain on PB's resources and action should be taken to correct this.

M2: PB is market leader for this product and is seeing an increase in profitability offset by increasing operating costs. The nearest competitor, however, seems to be more efficient in production resulting in a higher level of operating profit to turnover for both the years under review. Proportionately, the competitor's increase in operating costs is running at the level of 44% of the increase in turnover, whereas PB's comparative values show that its operating costs have increased by 53% of increased turnover levels between the two years. This leads to the view that the competitor is more efficient and although PB may be market leader now, this situation may not prevail for very long. Again, action needs to be taken to redress this trend.

M3: This is the "question mark" product moving towards a "star". Comparisons with the competitor reveal less clear cut evidence. PB's operating profit to turnover has declined while the competitor's has remained the same over the two years, but total turnover for both companies has increased. Similarly, the operating costs for both companies have increased.

The slightly better performance overall by the competitor in comparison with PB has led to what appears to be a startling improvement in pre-tax profit, but this is exaggerated by the low base figures. It is unclear what action should be taken with M3, which is always likely to be the case for a "question mark" product. PB needs to decide whether or not it wishes to risk sinking more resources into M3 with a view to converting it into a "star" and, ultimately, a "cash cow".

Requirement (c)

Evaluation of the best option

	M1	**M1**	**M1**	**Total**
	$m	*$m*	*$m*	*$m*
Option:				
Withdraw:				
Loss of profit (2004 level)	0·2	2·2	0·8	(3·2)
Loss of other profit				(4·0)
Incremental closure costs				(2·0)
Effect on Group pre-tax operating profit				(9·2)

> **Examiner's note:**
> The loss of profits at the 2004 level is known. It would have been equally acceptable if the calculation had shown the loss of profit at the projected 2005 level.

	M1	**M1**	**M1**	**Total**
	$m	*$m*	*$m*	*$m*
Maintain:				
Turnover	5·63	8·00	4·62	18·25
Operating costs	5·80	5·25	3·62	14·67
Pre-tax operating profit	(0·17)	2·75	1·00	3·58
Export:				
Turnover	5·63	8·00	4·62	18·25
Operating costs	6·12	5·51	3·80	(15·43)
Incremental closure costs				(2·00)
Transport costs				(1·00)
Effect on Group pre-tax operating profit				(0·18)
Licence:				
Income				2·0
Quality assurance costs				(0·5)
Incremental closure costs				(2·0)
Effect on Group pre-tax operating profit				(0·5)

> **Examiner's note:**
> This answer takes a total profit approach. It would have been acceptable for a differential profit approach to have been taken.

Commentary and recommendation:
Financially, the preferred option is to maintain the production facility PB in Bigland. However, product M1 is reducing in profitability and it is clear that there is inefficiency in the production of M2 and M3. Therefore, it is questionable how long PB will remain profitable at all. Given the low profitability for PB, the fact that the MD of the subsidiary has not arrested this decline and the anticipation that this will in fact get worse, the best option seems likely to face the situation now and close PB. In the short run it is recommended that the Bigland market be served by exporting products M2 and M3. As profitability reduces, these products may be strategically withdrawn and this will be easier to achieve through exporting rather than closing the plant when it becomes a forced sale. Product M1 should be discontinued altogether now.

This advice takes no account of any other market information which may be available in respect of Bigland.

Requirement (d)

The organisational structure of PB follows the classical approach of scientific management. It is traditional, but the company is encountering difficulties in respect of staff turnover. In addition, it appears that PB is finding it necessary to pay premium salaries and wages to attract staff. This, coupled with the increased recruitment and training costs, is likely to be one cause of its reducing profitability. A hidden direct cost of this, but one which is all too apparent in profit and loss terms, is the poor level of efficiency. It is necessary therefore, for action to be taken in respect of the company structure.

Review of each of the Chairman's options for PB results in the following organisational structural impacts being identified:

Withdraw
This will reduce the overhead costs for the company as a whole and it has a dramatic effect on the structure in that PB will simply cease to exist. This, however, will cause some human resource issues to be faced in respect of termination of staff contracts in Bigland. This may have adverse effects on staff morale elsewhere in the Group, as well as potentially damaging the reputation of the P Group in Bigland. Lessons of the shortcomings of the previous structure which was in place in PB should be learned by the P Group.

Maintain
If PB is to remain then the structure should be changed to improve staff morale and reduce costs. At the very least a more participative form of management needs to be adopted. The organisational structure needs to enable management to be more environmentally aware and encourage staff to communicate their thoughts. It may only be necessary to alter the style which would involve the removal of the present Managing Director of PB. However, a new MD appointment is likely to result in a revision to the structure possibly with a simple flat organisation. This may result in lateral communication and encouragement of innovation to solve problems. The benefits of this would be low managerial overheads and quicker decision making but an informal hierarchy may lead to confusion and leave strategic direction entirely a matter for the MD.

Exporting
The same organisational impacts as withdrawal will apply but in addition there will be a greater workload on the staff at the manufacturing plant from which the products are exported. This may require a change in structure at that plant. It may be necessary to develop a new division dedicated to the export of the products to Bigland. It is unlikely that the increased workload can simply be absorbed unless there is spare capacity in the exporting manufacturing plant. The export function is unlikely to be as aware of environmental changes in Bigland as would be expected from a direct investment in the country. This, however, may not be a serious issue to the P Group senior management if their intention ultimately is strategic withdrawal from the country.

Licence
Again there will be a major impact on the current structure of PB as there will no longer be a manufacturing plant, unless there is a management buyout. However, the senior management of the P Group will need to maintain its reputation for quality and may offer servicing contract support to the licensee. This will result in quality assurance personnel being engaged or sent to Bigland. These may be drawn from the current staff of PB. However, this is achieved the reporting arrangements and relationships between the quality assurance staff and the senior management of the P Group need to be clearly established.

SECTION B

Answer to Question Two

Requirement (a)

Approaches to strategy formulation

There are several ways of distinguishing approaches to strategy formulation, three are discussed here:

- The Rational approach
- The Emergent approach
- Logical incrementalism [0]

The textbook approach to strategy formulation is termed the *"rational approach"*. Here strategy appears to be consciously pre-planned and embraces a series of clear stages including:

- the establishment of the goals of the organisation (maybe expressed through mission and objectives);
- the conducting of a corporate appraisal that involves reviewing both internal factors as part of a position audit and external environmental factors;
- the identification of objectives;
- these objectives are evaluated and choices made;
- strategy implementation;
- the final significant element is a control mechanism that leads to a review of the organisation's position.

This deliberate, formal rational strategic process represents the traditional prescribed view of strategy development. It contains several implicit assumptions and as a model started to be challenged during the late 1970s. Observers noticed organisations diluted this rational model by, for instance, omitting key stages or pursuing hidden agendas. In any case, not all "successful" organisations appeared to adhere to this process.

A more *emergent view* of strategy development became recognised. Such a view was forged on the notion of a need for constant strategic adjustments and adaptation in order to survive in a hostile, fast moving external environment. Theorists viewed the oil crisis and the apparent success of Japanese businesses that did not appear to follow the prescribed view with curiosity. Thinkers such as Minzberg (1990) and Porter (1985) led the academic debate that proposed an alternative "way". (Mintzberg's classification of strategies being intended, deliberate, realised, unrealised and emergent).

[0] Johnson and Scholes (2003) capture strategic approaches in the form of three lenses or ways of thinking: design, experience and ideas. Whittington (2001) alternatively identifies four approaches:

classical, evolutionary, processual, and systemic.

Alternative classifications such as these may be adopted and will receive appropriate credit

Lindblom first used the term *"logical incrementalism"* in a negative way, while Quinn built on this thinking by identifying the management role as one of moving their organisations forward in small incremental steps, rather than relying on grand visions and rigid strategic plans. This might contain the following features:

- Individual managers co-ordinate a network of formal and informal communications with staff, customers and others so becoming aware of the issues confronting the organisation. (Formal strategy models and techniques might be used to conceptualise these).

- If change is required or events are influencing the organisation in a particular direction, they will start to develop a general overall vision. They are likely to wait until circumstances make others responsive to ideas for change.

- This means that rather than unveiling strategy explicitly, the manager will build support for ideas in a political way that avoids opposition and conflict.

- Gradually commitment grows through trials of the strategy and a consensus grows for this "new way".

In the case of SPK a rational approach to strategy is not appropriate as it would be seen as too rigid, formalised and probably counter productive. SPK partners and managers operate in an autonomous way "sensing" business opportunities and trading on reputation and knowledge and would not wish to compromise this to a formalised system of operating.

This means that alternative categorisations of strategy formulation approaches apply. The emergent approach is generally suited to a fast moving area of private sector. Although it seems that SPK strategic approaches are moulded and emerge based on experience there is no evidence from the question that SPK operates in a particularly fast moving environment.

For networked fluid organisations, logical incrementalism seems most appropriate. This could be seen to be the best fit for SPK for a number of reasons. Partners and senior managers are strong willed, highly opinionated and work independently of one another. It would be unwise to risk surfacing unwanted differences of opinion by unveiling a new strategy. (It may lead to a damaging and unwanted internal war that could be a distraction).

Partners and senior managers enjoy autonomy and they would undoubtedly resist attempts to restrict their power through a more formalised strategic approach. SPK places a lot of trust in its partners and senior managers and would not seek to undermine this. The SPK way is consistent with strategy development through political means in a logical, incremental way.

Senior partners could usefully contribute to this process;

- by looking to improve the quality of information used by managers and partners;
- by overcoming personal and political pressures;
- by building organisational awareness and support for strategies.

Only by moving incrementally and building a consensus can they effectively bring about strategic change.

Requirement (b)

Public sector organisations and strategy development

Unlike privately owned businesses, the public sector's main purpose is for social rather than financial reasons. For organisations such as hospitals, educational establishments and units of local government these social objectives can be multiple and contradictory. (For example, a need to reduce hospital bed stay to free up beds but conversely reduce the cost of post discharge health costs, or increase educational provision, but seek to reduce levels of taxation, and so on.)

This means that the setting of objectives and their measurement is more problematic and traditional financial performance measures cannot be easily applied. Additionally, rather than exist for owners or shareholders, public sector organisations exist to serve a wider range of stakeholders. It follows that strategic processes need to be explicit, deliberate and involve or consider stakeholders. (If comparison is drawn to SPK their objectives are straightforward:

- profitability; and
- reputation maintenance.

(The dominant stakeholders to satisfy are the senior partners).

As they are funded from public funds, public sector organisations owe a duty of stewardship to society demonstrated through a process of public accountability. Here they must justify that they have acted in a logical, thoughtful way. The rational approach is well suited to demonstrating such a process. The "hunch and lunch" approach of SPK could not be justified for a public sector organisation as a democratically accountable body.

In addition, the direct requirements of Central Government can be more easily factored in as part of a logical methodical approach.

Public sector organisations come under much external scrutiny. Public interest in behaviour, and the careful public monitoring by politicians and the media means it must be seen to deliver strategy fairly and properly, and the rational planning process provides such a mechanism whereby strategy is clear and political opinions made explicit.

In summary, strategy formulation in public sector organisations is shaped by a number of distinctive characteristics differences not least wider stakeholder involvement, limited resources and central political priorities. The rational model can accommodate these features to good effect.

Performance measurement

Criticisms of the public sector often stem from its very nature. A lack of direct competition means no comparison of performance is easily made. The lack of a profit motive can lead to suggestions that they are not interested in cost reduction or that services provided have little incentive to be improved upon. The public sector must therefore demonstrate value for money in the use of the resources they have available to them.

For effective performance management, the overall aims and objectives of the service should be clarified. These will allow reasonable expectations to be developed. The views of all the stakeholders, once known, can be incorporated into the strategic planning process. Decision makers can then ensure that methods of assessing performance are appropriate. One framework for setting objectives and subsequently assessing performance as a form of stewardship is suggested as focussing on the three Es; Economy, Efficiency and Effectiveness.

Economy relates to resource acquisition or inputs. Thus issues of cost of purchase or operations commensurate with quality arise. Efficiency is the process stage whereby the resources are used to produce outputs. What the organisation "does" to transform the inputs and what it could have done better are immediate concerns. Finally, effectiveness looks back to original objectives and considers success at meeting these aspirations.

Indicators of performance can be developed in the form of ratios and so on, and these can be used in conjunction with intra organisational comparisons (for example similar sites or departments within the same body), or historical patterns and trends can be developed. There has been over the past ten years or so within the UK a growing trend towards the use of multiple performance indicators and ratios and the publication of these in the form of "league tables" of organisations. Thus, a form of inter-organisational benchmarking is being pursued. These exercises ensure that the levels of cost and service can be compared with the inputs, processes and outputs of similar service providers. Managers, elected representatives, auditors and more generally the public, can glean insights of "good practice" and areas for improvement. One of the difficulties of this is that indicators, rather than forming the basis for further investigation, get treated as absolute measures. The simplistic accumulation of indicators into league tables worsens this situation. It is likely, however, that some form of comparison and measurement of performance will bring about value for money improvements in economy, efficiency and effectiveness.

Answer to Question Three

Requirement (a)

The role performed by PFM and the source of its power and apparent interest

PFM acting on behalf of its investors represents a powerful stakeholder as an active shareholder grouping. It has the will and implied experience to intervene where necessary and bring pressure for changes. This means that the Chairman and Board can now be called to account in a more direct way than ever before.

Is it legitimate for PFM to act in this way? Clearly PFM is legally entitled to do so as an owner of the company. Directors <u>should</u> be accountable to shareholders as part of a process of corporate governance. PFM is taking this right one stage further than most other investors. A number of key questions arise such as:

- Is PFM "stretching" its own rights too fully?
- Are the people on whose behalf PFM is investing comfortable with the way in which it is acting?
- In any case, is PFM's judgment valid?

Mendelow (1991) proposed a 2x2 cell matrix (the power-interest matrix) to help analyse stakeholders. Here PFM would be classified as both powerful and interested and according to Mendelow needs to be "kept informed" of strategy. A particular strategic development needs to be carefully thought through in the light of PFM's stance. Boards of directors would ignore PFM at their peril.

When assessing the indicators of power of stakeholders a number of factors might usefully be considered, including:

- status of the stakeholders, (for example place in the organisational hierarchy; relative pay; reputation; social standing and so on.);
- claim or control on resources, (for example size of budget; number and level of staff employed; volume of business transacted; percentage of workers they speak for, and son on.);
- formal representation in decision-making processes, (for example level in hierarchy of management; bodies they have representation on; legal rights);
- possession of knowledge and skills.

For external stakeholders in particular it may be control of strategic resource (materials, labour, money), involvement in strategy implementation (for example distribution outlets, agents), possession of knowledge or skills (such as that enjoyed by subcontractors) and internal links and informal influence.
In the case of PFM the basis is control of finance and potential willingness to be involved in strategy based upon implied skills and knowledge.

The interest of stakeholders will be more complex because it involves two factors; where their interests rest and how interested they are. Powerful stakeholders generally will pursue their self-interest, therefore, what they wish to achieve is of significance. (For instance, employees require higher pay, job security, good working conditions and some consultation and so on.) Not all stakeholders have the time or inclination to follow management's decisions closely. This is not so for PFM which explicitly does show interest to a degree that few other stakeholders can match. Its requirement is also explicitly stated.

Requirement (b)

Putting in place performance evaluation and incentive systems to provide managers with incentive to deliver long term shareholder value

Shareholder value is understood as (Corporate value – Debt), where corporate value is the present value of cash flows from activities over the forecast period plus residual cash inflows at the period end, for example scrap value of sold assets (Rappaport 1998). Therefore to increase shareholder value, managers must at all times be using the assets at their disposal in activities that yield a positive NPV over the forecast period. This applies throughout a firm and means, for instance, that before embarking on an advertising campaign the marketing manager must be reasonably sure that the increased revenues from higher sales must provide an NPV against the money ploughed into the campaign. In brief, "quick gains" to boost profits, or make the figures "look good" should not be at the expense of the long term interests of the company.

In the scenario in the question, PFM would be keen to monitor these factors.

The issue therefore arises as to how to implement incentive systems so that they stimulate managers to act in a way that does not hurt shareholder value. Simply by operating measures of longer-term performance some progress can be achieved. The measures themselves can act as a stimulus in a number of ways. Measurement indicates what is important. Managers are likely to modify behaviour to meet these targets. This is particularly so if it is embodied as a factor in the staff appraisal systems as measures make explicit what is important.

Measurement may be linked to a second HR system; the reward system. It may form part of an incentive pay bonus scheme. Alternatively, it might be criteria for promotion.

The tradition of rewarding managers for financial performance such as meeting budgetary targets is well established. The organisation should determine the precise metrics that are important, both financial and non financial and link rewards to performance accordingly.

Some easily identifiable stages emerge in developing appropriate internal measures for the activities of the business:

- Identify the key outputs required. This is determined by stakeholder demands and may be found in the mission or objectives of the business unit/division.
- Identify the processes in providing the outputs through discussions with management and staff, and so on.
- Identify relationships to activities in other parts of the firm. These activities will be outside a person's control.
- Develop performance indicators for the key processes (KPIs).
- Identify data sources for measures.
- Develop a reporting system.
- Review effectiveness of the control system.

Answer to Question Four

Requirement (a)

Glaspac's position and options

Gap analysis involves comparison between an organisation's ultimate objective and the expected performance of both planned and on-going projects in meeting this objective. Any shortfall leads to examination of performance and resource requirement.

If there is a consequent gap between stated objectives and forecast performance, then the organisation has two options; either revise the stated objectives or put in place strategies that will close the strategic gap. In order to determine the most appropriate strategy to meet forecast performance it is necessary to first understand the causes of the "gap".

The potential market demand is $400,000 and existing sales are $300,000. This means that there is a gap of $100,000. Analysis of the reasons for the gap may suggest the areas to address with new policies. For instance:

- A "Demand" gap: the difference between total market potential and current demand. The "gap" may be because the market is nervous at the moment of entering into financing deals. This may be as a result of external factors outside the company's control, for instance fluctuations in interest rates. To close the gap some form of marketing/ advertising campaign may be necessary, or prices could be reduced. The company may wish for instance to offer low rate financing deals. This may help bridge the planning gap but will have implications for profitability.

- A "Distribution" gap is a loss of product demand due to lack of access to distribution channels. Glaspac displays products and gives out promotional literature in shopping malls and large stores in the area. Does it still have access to sufficient sites? Are there new malls and stores and areas that Glaspac does not have access to? Glaspac may comprehensively rethink how it gets its products onto the market, maybe newspaper advertising or national television or radio commercials might be more effective?

- A "Product" gap (a proportion of market demand is lost through product failure). Product returns and faulty work may mean that Glaspac is starting to acquire an unfavourable reputation and that is impacting on sales. Alternatively, the product design and range may be viewed as outdated and less attractive than their rivals. Actions could include reviewing the portfolio in terms of product quality, range and style and modifying products accordingly.

- A "Competitive" gap normally results in a loss in sales. In this case there has been a fall of at least $50,000 from two years ago. What this means is that Glaspac is being outperformed by the competition. Under these circumstances they may wish to consider its existing pricing and promotion strategies.

It is highly likely that the gap is as a result of a combination of these factors and/or an over ambitious estimate of $400,000.

In all deliberations it is important to think beyond the immediate target of sales to other measures not least profitability. In other words it is important that the decision makers are not blinded by this one technique but, instead, try to build a coherent picture of the strategic position it finds itself in.

> **Examiner's note:**
> The use of other approaches, such as Ansoff's matrix, are acceptable.

Requirement (b)

Relationship between planning gap and scenario plans and how they might be used together

Scenario plans are used by some organisations in the planning stage to develop future plausible "situations" or scenarios from key uncertainties and known facts and trends. The organisation can then consider how it might position itself with regard to each scenario. Key triggers to such hypothetical situations can be identified and then monitored in practice in order to have an early warning of events described within the scenario becoming reality.

Gap analysis follows on from an analysis of an organisation's portfolio of products and services, which represent the interface between itself and the external environment.

Both scenario planning and gap analysis are based upon known facts, existing trends and form part of the evaluation of strategic options. Both use what is known at present and make future projections. They also draw on the knowledge and expertise of the workforce. If used collaboratively they can lead to a buy in to strategies and increase motivation and teamwork.

Gap analysis can provoke discussion by taking account of a range of potential situations that might arise in the future (so borrowing from scenario planning). One way in which discussions could be framed would be around scenarios and implications upon sales in two years time if (for instance);

- there is no change in competition;
- competitors working in alliances with one another cause an effect;
- a major new entrant to the market place provides effective competition;

This could stimulate a debate about the range of sales levels two years hence, and the types of actions that would be needed to fill the planning gap (see diagram).

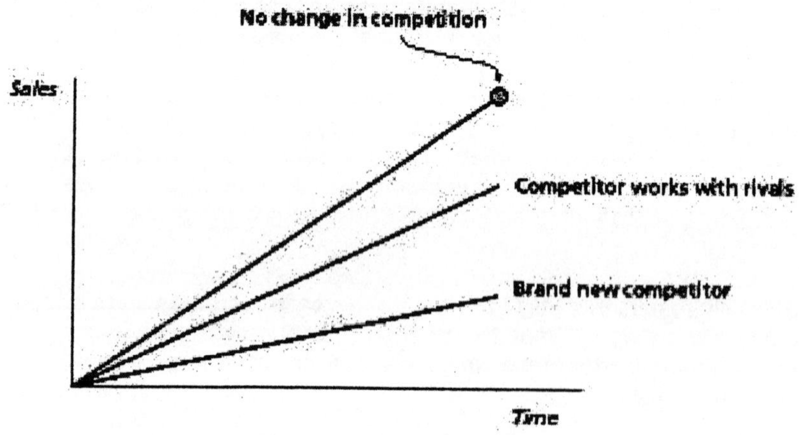

Organisations when faced with multiple scenarios may choose to:

- decide which scenario is most likely and plan its strategy accordingly. This could form the basis of gap analysis projections (possibly not the $400,000 identified);
- have ready-made strategies for deployment at short notice as triggering events occur. In the case of Glaspac the merger of two of its rivals might be one such event;
- concentrate on developing core competences (in the case of Glaspac its added security features) that can sustain the organisation irrespective of the scenario.

Answer to Question Five

Requirement (a)

Virtual networked organisations; key strategic issues as potential strategic strengths or weaknesses

Many online service companies now exist with examples to be found in publishing and specialist travel. Most famously perhaps is Amazon.com which claims to be "the premier international retailer of books, music, and movies". The buyer is offered an "online store, reliable shipping and delivery, and renowned customer service". Yet Amazon's continued operation is in marked contrast to the number of other dot.com companies who have since gone out of business. (Amazon, incidentally, until recently consistently failed to make a net profit). There are many critics of virtual companies because of their perceived inherent strategic weaknesses and Charles Handy (1996) once described them rather dismissively as a "bag of contracts". Undeniably, virtual organisations can display a number of strengths, including flexibility, focus, potential for quick growth and asset efficiency.

The key issue appears to be how well relationships within and outside the organisation are fostered and maintained. This implies particular skills to build and then enrich a range of relationships. If this skill is present it will translate as strength. If not it will be a weakness. The company is only as good as the sub-contractors who work on its behalf. The reliability of sub-contractors is tested in emergencies and when things "go wrong". Multiple suppliers in any case may be difficult to manage effectively. The systems and expertise to cope with such relationships may not be in place (representing a weakness). Alternatively, if this expertise is present it will be a strength.

One key relationship is that with the customer. The organisation may be virtual, but it needs to "feel" real to customers in order for them to transact business. The customer needs reassurance that, for instance, credit card details are secure. The livery of vehicles, packaging of products and badging of services can help overcome concerns about the reality of the business and therefore credibility of the organisation. The issue of a lack of staff to back up service could be a persistent weakness. In summary, the health of customer relationship will translate into either a strategic strength or weakness.

If the organisation meets the needs of the customer (and supplier) as adequately as traditional organisational forms then there will be no difficulty. The organisation, however, must have at least a threshold industry competence otherwise this will be a strategic weakness.

Critics claim that most virtual operations are devoid of core competences and this will lead to serious strategic weaknesses in the long run. If the organisation does identify a core competence this is clearly a strategic strength.

Undeniably highly networked organisations are cut off from the learning of performing some activities in house. In other words, they see the organisation as a series of contracts and operations and fail to gain a holistic overview. The key challenge for the virtual organisation is how to integrate pockets of knowledge that exist to bring about organisational learning. Without this challenge being addressed, an organisation would show a strategic weakness as a lack of capacity for innovation.

Requirement (b)

Environmental analysis and what are the difficulties in an organization that is highly networked

The environmental analysis has alternatively been described as "external auditing" or "scanning" and relates to the collection of information on the environment within which an organisation operates. (It is acknowledged at this point that the degree of usage of environmental information varies enormously from organisation to organisation).

Benefits of the process include:

- Provides information to help formulate strategy.
- Helps give a competitive advantage by identifying opportunities in the environment.
- Provides a base of objective qualitative information.
- Encourages sensitivity to changing customer's demands.
- Acts as stimulus for strategy makers.
- Improves public standing by demonstrating sensitivity to the environment.
- Provides an on going forum of development for managers and strategists.

(Jain,1990)

With the external environment becoming more chaotic and complex, networked organisations may have grown as a response to this. It is something of a paradox therefore, that it might be less easy to obtain information about this chaotic environment in these new structures than in traditionally structured organisations.

Potentially, environmental scanning occurs at three discernible levels, line management, strategic planning and a specialist function. In the case of the highly networked organisation this delineation will not be as apparent and the process may not be conducted unless alternative scanning approaches are considered.

Data collection in more traditional organisational structures encourages a broader participation in the business strategy process. For network organisations this wider involvement that arguably produces better strategy will not be available. Thus, the whole organisation's future is more dependent upon the thought processes and judgements of a few key people.

In order to generate up-to-date databases of information for dissemination to decision makers, it is important to capture all possible knowledge sources. For an organisation that is highly networked with few staff, an important source of potential knowledge is denied. This "soft" knowledge that can be generated by day-to-day conversations and through regular management meetings will not be so readily available. The networked organisation should seek to provide a substitute for this deficiency, maybe in the form of (say) organising supplier or contractor forums by using an external consultant or by organising focus group meetings. Where strategic alliances are forged, efforts should be made to take advantage of the potential richness of human relationships and interactions (albeit that issues of confidentiality may arise).

CIMA

November 2004 Examinations

Final Level

Management Accounting – Financial Strategy

(FLFS – Paper 13)

The answers published here have been written by the Examiner and should provide a helpful guide for both lecturers and students.

Published separately on the CIMA website (www.cimaglobal.com/students) from the end of March 2005 is a Post Examination Guide for this paper, which provides much valuable and complementary material including indicative mark information.

CIMA

Final Level

Management Accounting – Financial Strategy

13 FLFS

23 November 2004

Tuesday afternoon

INSTRUCTIONS TO CANDIDATES

Read this page before you look at the questions

You are allowed three hours to answer this question paper.
Answer the ONE question in Section A. Answer TWO questions ONLY from Section B.
Maths Tables and Formulae are provided.

SECTION A – 50 MARKS

READ THE SCENARIO AND ANSWER THE QUESTION

Question One

Background
RGB is a computer technology business based in the UK. It was listed until 4 years ago but following disagreements between the Board and major shareholders, the directors and senior managers bought out the external shareholders, effectively re-privatising the company.

RGB sells its products and services worldwide, but its main market outside the UK is in North America. To date, all its manufacturing and administrative functions have been conducted from the UK.

Summary Financial Statements for last financial year

	£m
Turnover	840
Earnings (post-tax)	76
Fixed assets	650
Net current assets	90
Less: Long term liabilities	
(8% Secured loan repayable 2010)	(320)
Total net assets	420
Shareholders' equity	420
(120 million £1 shares in issue)	

The average P/E ratio of listed companies in a similar industry is 10·53.

Company objectives
The company has three stated objectives. These are:

- Increase earnings per share by 5% per annum;
- Post-tax accounting rate of return on shareholders' funds of 20% per annum;
- Maintain a leading global presence in its operating markets.

New Capital Investment
The company is evaluating establishing a new manufacturing plant, marketing and administration facility in either the South of England or North America. Ideally, it would like to open the new UK facility as well as expanding into North America, but it does not believe it has the financial or management resources to do both at the same time.

RGB has a policy of limiting capital investment in any one financial year to £50 million. Last year the company did not spend up to this limit, however capital investments have already been approved in the current year that require total capital expenditure of £17 million. None of these can be postponed without loss of money spent on set up costs such as feasibility studies.

The estimated cost for the UK investment is £30 million. These initial investment costs will be written off over a period of 5 years. To establish operations in North America will cost an estimated US$75 million. This US investment, combined with capital expenditure already committed, would exceed the company's capital investment limit if it were to be enforced.

Forecast pre-tax operating nominal cash flows for the first three years of operations are as follows:

Year		*1*	*2*	*3*
North America Investment	US$m	22·25	24·25	26·25
UK	£m	6·30	9·00	10·50

- All operating cash flows may be assumed to occur at the end of each year. The initial capital investment will be made at the beginning of year 1 (year 0).
- Estimated cash flows beyond year 3 are highly uncertain, but for purposes of evaluation, the company assumes 5% per year growth on year 3's pre-tax operating sterling cash flows until the end of year 5. Cash flows beyond year 5 are ignored.

The investments this year will be financed by cash. The company has built up cash reserves of £50 million over the past 2 years and has also recently agreed the cash sale of some surplus assets.

Exchange rate information

	Forecast inflation rates per annum constant
USA	1·5%
UK	2·5%

The spot $/£ exchange rate as at today is 1·70.

Taxation
Corporate tax rates in the two countries are as follows:

USA	25%
UK	30%

Assume for the purposes of evaluation:

- Both countries allow 100% first year allowance tax relief on capital investments of this type.
- There is a double taxation treaty in existence.
- Tax is payable (or refundable) at the end of the year in which the liability or refund arises.
- RGB pays tax at the national tax rates.

Cost of capital and adjustment for risk
For domestic investments RGB uses a risk-adjusted discount rate using the CAPM where possible. The expected nominal, post-tax risk free rate in the UK is 5% and the return on the market is 9%. The quoted equity beta of a suitable proxy company with similar capital structure to RGB is 1·3.

However, RGB's Finance Director recognises that the risks involved in the overseas proposal are different. Determining an appropriate discount rate to reflect risk is difficult in the circumstances. She has therefore recommended that the post-tax cash flows for the North American venture be adjusted using estimates of probability applied to sterling cash flows, discounted at the risk free rate. These estimates of probability are as follows:

Year:	*1*	*2*	*3*
Probability	0·9	0·87	0·82

Beyond year 3, a probability factor of 0·7 is estimated.

Methods of investment appraisal
RGB uses NPV analysis in the investment appraisal process, but the company also expects new investments to contribute to all the company's objectives.

Required:

Assume you are the Capital Investment Analyst at RGB.

(a) Estimate the discount rate to be used in the evaluation of the UK investment and comment briefly on the limitations of using this rate in the investment being proposed here for RGB. Assume RGB's debt is trading at par and has a beta of zero.

(5 marks)

(b) Calculate the NPV, Profitability Index and estimated Accounting Rate of Return on Capital Employed (ROCE) for each investment. For the purposes of calculating the ROCE, assume that cumulative sterling post-tax cash flows at the end of year 5 equal cumulative post-tax profits before depreciation.

(20 marks)

(c) Write a report to the board evaluating the proposed investments. Include the following sections in your report:

(i) An evaluation of how each of the two investments will contribute to the achievement of the company's stated objectives;

(10 marks)

(ii) An analysis of the various types of risk involved in these investments and advice on a strategy for managing those risks. Include comments on the methods the Finance Director has recommended to adjust the cash flows for risk;

(8 marks)

(iii) A recommendation as to whether the company should invest in either or both projects. Include comments on the appropriateness of RGB limiting investment to £50 million in the current financial year.

(7 marks)

(Total for part (c) = 25 marks)

(Total = 50 marks)

SECTION B – 50 MARKS

ANSWER TWO QUESTIONS ONLY

Question Two

TLC Inc manufactures pharmaceutical products. The organisation exports through a worldwide network of affiliated organisations. Its headquarters are in the USA, but there is a large volume of inter-organisation sales, dividend flows and fee and royalty payments. These inter-organisational payments are made in US$. An example of payment flows among four affiliates for the past 6 months is shown on the diagram below:

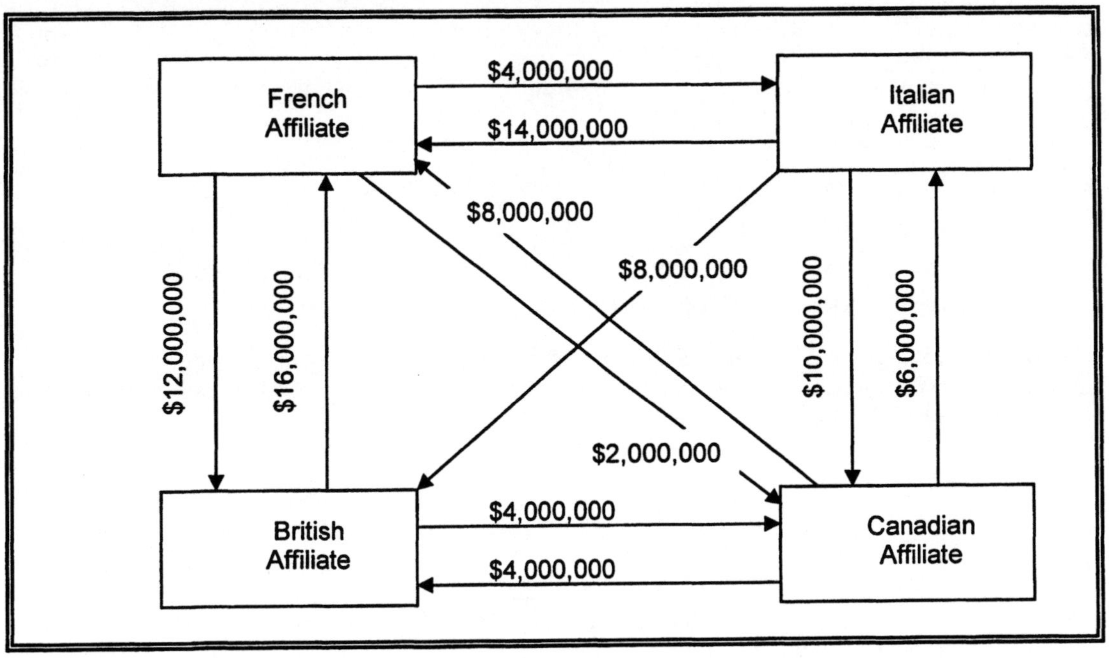

At present, each affiliate has control over its own cash management and foreign currency hedging decisions. The Corporate Treasurer is considering centralising cash and foreign currency management.

Required:

(a) Explain, briefly, the characteristics of a bi- or multi-lateral netting system and, using the information in the diagram, advise the Corporate Treasurer of the pattern of cash flows that would have been evident if such a system had been in operation in TLC Inc.

(12 marks)

(b) Discuss the advantages TLC Inc might obtain from centralising international cash management and foreign exchange management and advise on the potential disadvantages of such a change in policy.

(13 marks)

(Total = 25 marks)

A report format is not required for this question.

Question Three

AB and YZ both operate department stores in Europe. They operate in similar markets and are generally considered to be direct competitors. Both companies have had similar earnings records over the past ten years and have similar capital structures. The earnings and dividend record of the two companies over the past six years is as follows:

	AB			YZ		
Year to 31 March	*EPS cents*	*DPS cents*	*Average share price cents*	*EPS cents*	*DPS cents*	*Average share price cents*
1999	230	60	2100	240	96	2200
2000	150	60	1500	160	64	1700
2001	100	60	1000	90	36	1400
2002	-125	60	800	-110	0	908
2003	100	60	1000	90	36	1250
2004	150	60	1400	145	58	1700

Note: EPS = Earnings per Share and DPS = Dividends per Share

AB has had 25 million shares in issue for the past six years. YZ currently has 25 million shares in issue. At the beginning of 2003 YZ had a 1 for 4 rights issue. The EPS and DPS have been adjusted in the above table.

The Chairman of AB is concerned that the share price of YZ is higher than his company's, despite the fact that AB has recently earned more per share than YZ and frequently during the past six years has paid a higher dividend.

Required:

(a) Discuss:

(i) the apparent dividend policy followed by each company over the past 6 years and comment on the possible relationship of these policies to the companies' market values and current share prices; and

(ii) whether there is an optimal dividend policy for AB that might increase shareholder value.

(12 marks)

(b) Forecast earnings for AB for the year to 31 March 2005 are €40 million. At present, it has excess cash of €2·5 million and is considering a share repurchase in addition to maintaining last year's dividend. The Chairman thinks this will have a number of benefits for the company, including a positive effect on the share price.

Advise the Chairman of AB of

- how a share repurchase may be arranged;
- the main reasons for a share repurchase;
- the potential problems of such an action, compared with a one-off extra dividend payment, and any possible effect on the share price of AB.

(13 marks)

(Total = 25 marks)

A report format is not required for this question.

Question Four

GH Organisation is based in Germany. It has one subsidiary based in the UK, accounting for 35% of GH's total business. GH Organisation has borrowings of €15 million at a fixed rate of 6% per annum and £10 million sterling at a variable rate of LIBOR + 2%. LIBOR is currently 6% per annum. Interest is payable on both loans annually and is due to be paid in 6 months' time.

Interest and inflation rates (per annum)

	UK	*European Common Currency Area (ECCA)*	*USA*
Central bank base rates	5·0%	3·5%	3·0%
Inflation rates (Forecast by Central Bank)	2·5%	1·5%	1·0%

Exchange rates	*€/£*	*€/US$*
Current quoted spot rates	1·8100	1·0000
3 month forward rates	1·8033	

The Chief Executive of GH Organisation has asked you as Assistant Treasurer to answer the following questions:

1 What are the real costs to us at present of borrowing, in both Euros and £ Sterling, in terms of annual interest rates?

2 As we are currently considering raising new capital should we look at borrowing in Euros (Eurobonds perhaps?) or Sterling, or a third currency such as the US$?

3 What are the various methods available to us to manage our interest rate risk?

4 Interest is payable in 6 months' time. What amount are we likely to have to pay on our sterling loans, and should we consider hedging the amount, for example by using a forward contract?

5 Would it be more advantageous to borrow at fixed or floating rate given our present circumstances?

Required:

Write a memorandum to the Chief Executive replying to his queries, providing a full explanation of the issues he raises accompanied by relevant and appropriate calculations.

(Total = 25 marks)

Marks are split roughly equally between sections of this question.

Question Five

BST Motors plc (BST) is a long-established listed company. Its main business is the retailing of new and used motor cars and the provision of after-sales service. It has sales outlets in most of the major towns and cities in the UK. It also owns a substantial amount of land and property that it has acquired over the years, much of which it rents or leases on medium-long term agreements. Approximately 80% of its fixed asset value is land and buildings.

The company has grown organically for the last few years but is now considering expanding by acquisition. The Chief Executive is not in favour of hostile bids as he believes the bidder always pays too much to acquire the target. Any acquisition that BST makes will therefore need to be an agreed bid.

SM Limited (SM) owns a number of car showrooms in wealthy, semi-rural locations in the North of England. All of these showrooms operate the franchise of a well-known major motor manufacturer. SM is a long-established private company with the majority of shares owned by the founding family, many of whom still work for the company. The major shareholders are now considering selling the business if a suitable price can be agreed. The Managing Director of SM, who is a major shareholder, has approached BST to see if they would be interested in buying SM. He has implied that holders of up to 50% of SM's shares might be willing to accept BST shares as part of the deal.

The forecast earnings of BST for the next financial year are £35 million. According to the Managing Director of SM, his company's earnings are expected to be £4 million for the next financial year.

Financial statistics and other information on BST and SM are shown below:

	BST	*SM*
Shares in issue (millions)	25	1·5
Earnings per share (pence)	112·5	153
Dividend per share (pence)	50·6	100
Share price (pence)	1237	n/a
Net asset value attributable to equity (£m)	350	45
Debt ratio (outstanding debt as percentage of total market value of company)	20	0
Forecast growth rate percentage (constant, annualised)	4	5
Cost of equity	9%	n/a

SM does not calculate a cost of equity, but the industry average for similar companies is 10%

Required:

Assume you are a financial manager working with BST. Advise the BST Board on the following issues in connection with a possible bid for SM:

(i) Methods of valuation that might be appropriate and a range of valuations for SM within which BST should be prepared to negotiate;

(10 marks)

(ii) The financial factors relating to both companies that might affect the bid;

(5 marks)

(iii) The most appropriate form of funding the bid and the likely financial effects on BST;

(5 marks)

(iv) The advantages and disadvantages of growth by agreed acquisition as compared with growth by internal (or organic) investment.

(5 marks)

(Total = 25 marks)

A report format is not required for this question.

End of paper

Maths Tables and Formulae follow

MATHS TABLES AND FORMULAE

MATHS TABLES

Present value table

Present value of 1·00 unit of currency, that is $(1+r)^{-n}$ where r = interest rate; n = number of periods until payment or receipt.

Periods (n)	Interest rates (r) 1%	2%	3%	4%	5%	6%	7%	8%	9%	10%
1	0.990	0.980	0.971	0.962	0.952	0.943	0.935	0.926	0.917	0.909
2	0.980	0.961	0.943	0.925	0.907	0.890	0.873	0.857	0.842	0.826
3	0.971	0.942	0.915	0.889	0.864	0.840	0.816	0.794	0.772	0.751
4	0.961	0.924	0.888	0.855	0.823	0.792	0.763	0.735	0.708	0.683
5	0.951	0.906	0.863	0.822	0.784	0.747	0.713	0.681	0.650	0.621
6	0.942	0.888	0.837	0.790	0.746	0705	0.666	0.630	0.596	0.564
7	0.933	0.871	0.813	0.760	0.711	0.665	0.623	0.583	0.547	0.513
8	0.923	0.853	0.789	0.731	0.677	0.627	0.582	0.540	0.502	0.467
9	0.914	0.837	0.766	0.703	0.645	0.592	0.544	0.500	0.460	0.424
10	0.905	0.820	0.744	0.676	0.614	0.558	0.508	0.463	0.422	0.386
11	0.896	0.804	0.722	0.650	0.585	0.527	0.475	0.429	0.388	0.350
12	0.887	0.788	0.701	0.625	0.557	0.497	0.444	0.397	0.356	0.319
13	0.879	0.773	0.681	0.601	0.530	0.469	0.415	0.368	0.326	0.290
14	0.870	0.758	0.661	0.577	0.505	0.442	0.388	0.340	0.299	0.263
15	0.861	0.743	0.642	0.555	0.481	0.417	0.362	0.315	0.275	0.239
16	0.853	0.728	0.623	0.534	0.458	0.394	0.339	0.292	0.252	0.218
17	0.844	0.714	0.605	0.513	0.436	0.371	0.317	0.270	0.231	0.198
18	0.836	0.700	0.587	0.494	0.416	0.350	0.296	0.250	0.212	0.180
19	0.828	0.686	0.570	0.475	0.396	0.331	0.277	0.232	0.194	0.164
20	0.820	0.673	0.554	0.456	0.377	0.312	0.258	0.215	0.178	0.149

Periods (n)	Interest rates (r) 11%	12%	13%	14%	15%	16%	17%	18%	19%	20%
1	0.901	0.893	0.885	0.877	0.870	0.862	0.855	0.847	0.840	0.833
2	0.812	0.797	0.783	0.769	0.756	0.743	0.731	0.718	0.706	0.694
3	0.731	0.712	0.693	0.675	0.658	0.641	0.624	0.609	0.593	0.579
4	0.659	0.636	0.613	0.592	0.572	0.552	0.534	0.516	0.499	0.482
5	0.593	0.567	0.543	0.519	0.497	0.476	0.456	0.437	0.419	0.402
6	0.535	0.507	0.480	0.456	0.432	0.410	0.390	0.370	0.352	0.335
7	0.482	0.452	0.425	0.400	0.376	0.354	0.333	0.314	0.296	0.279
8	0.434	0.404	0.376	0.351	0.327	0.305	0.285	0.266	0.249	0.233
9	0.391	0.361	0.333	0.308	0.284	0.263	0.243	0.225	0.209	0.194
10	0.352	0.322	0.295	0.270	0.247	0.227	0.208	0.191	0.176	0.162
11	0.317	0.287	0.261	0.237	0.215	0.195	0.178	0.162	0.148	0.135
12	0.286	0.257	0.231	0.208	0.187	0.168	0.152	0.137	0.124	0.112
13	0.258	0.229	0.204	0.182	0.163	0.145	0.130	0.116	0.104	0.093
14	0.232	0.205	0.181	0.160	0.141	0.125	0.111	0.099	0.088	0.078
15	0.209	0.183	0.160	0.140	0.123	0.108	0.095	0.084	0.079	0.065
16	0.188	0.163	0.141	0.123	0.107	0.093	0.081	0.071	0.062	0.054
17	0.170	0.146	0.125	0.108	0.093	0.080	0.069	0.060	0.052	0.045
18	0.153	0.130	0.111	0.095	0.081	0.069	0.059	0.051	0.044	0.038
19	0.138	0.116	0.098	0.083	0.070	0.060	0.051	0.043	0.037	0.031
20	0.124	0.104	0.087	0.073	0.061	0.051	0.043	0.037	0.031	0.026

Cumulative present value of 1·00 unit of currency per annum, Receivable or Payable at the end of each year for *n* years $\frac{1-(1+r)^{-n}}{r}$

Periods	Interest rates (*r*)									
(*n*)	1%	2%	3%	4%	5%	6%	7%	8%	9%	10%
1	0.990	0.980	0.971	0.962	0.952	0.943	0.935	0.926	0.917	0.909
2	1.970	1.942	1.913	1.886	1.859	1.833	1.808	1.783	1.759	1.736
3	2.941	2.884	2.829	2.775	2.723	2.673	2.624	2.577	2.531	2.487
4	3.092	3.808	3.717	3.630	3.546	3.465	3.387	3.312	3.240	3.170
5	4.853	4.713	4.580	4.452	4.329	4.212	4.100	3.993	3.890	3.791
6	5.795	5.601	5.417	5.242	5.076	4.917	4.767	4.623	4.486	4.355
7	6.728	6.472	6.230	6.002	5.786	5.582	5.389	5.206	5.033	4.868
8	7.652	7.325	7.020	6.733	6.463	6.210	5.971	5.747	5.535	5.335
9	8.566	8.162	7.786	7.435	7.108	6.802	6.515	6.247	5.995	5.759
10	9.471	8.983	8.530	8.111	7.722	7.360	7.024	6.710	6.418	6.145
11	10.368	9.787	9.253	8.760	8.306	7.887	7.499	7.139	6.805	6.495
12	11.255	10.575	9.954	9.385	8.863	8.384	7.943	7.536	7.161	6.814
13	12.134	11.348	10.635	9.986	9.394	8.853	8.358	7.904	7.487	7.103
14	13.004	12.106	11.296	10.563	9.899	9.295	8.745	8.244	7.786	7.367
15	13.865	12.849	11.938	11.118	10.380	9.712	9.108	8.559	8.061	7.606
16	14.718	13.578	12.561	11.652	10.838	10.106	9.447	8.851	8.313	7.824
17	15.562	14.292	13.166	12.166	11.274	10.477	9.763	9.122	8.544	8.022
18	16.398	14.992	13.754	12.659	11.690	10.828	10.059	9.372	8.756	8.201
19	17.226	15.679	14.324	13.134	12.085	11.158	10.336	9.604	8.950	8.365
20	18.046	16.351	14.878	13.590	12.462	11.470	10.594	9.818	9.129	8.514

Periods	Interest rates (*r*)									
(*n*)	11%	12%	13%	14%	15%	16%	17%	18%	19%	20%
1	0.901	0.893	0.885	0.877	0.870	0.862	0.855	0.847	0.840	0.833
2	1.713	1.690	1.668	1.647	1.626	1.605	1.585	1.566	1.547	1.528
3	2.444	2.402	2.361	2.322	2.283	2.246	2.210	2.174	2.140	2.106
4	3.102	3.037	2.974	2.914	2.855	2.798	2.743	2.690	2.639	2.589
5	3.696	3.605	3.517	3.433	3.352	3.274	3.199	3.127	3.058	2.991
6	4.231	4.111	3.998	3.889	3.784	3.685	3.589	3.498	3.410	3.326
7	4.712	4.564	4.423	4.288	4.160	4.039	3.922	3.812	3.706	3.605
8	5.146	4.968	4.799	4.639	4.487	4.344	4.207	4.078	3.954	3.837
9	5.537	5.328	5.132	4.946	4.772	4.607	4.451	4.303	4.163	4.031
10	5.889	5.650	5.426	5.216	5.019	4.833	4.659	4.494	4.339	4.192
11	6.207	5.938	5.687	5.453	5.234	5.029	4.836	4.656	4.486	4.327
12	6.492	6.194	5.918	5.660	5.421	5.197	4.988	7.793	4.611	4.439
13	6.750	6.424	6.122	5.842	5.583	5.342	5.118	4.910	4.715	4.533
14	6.982	6.628	6.302	6.002	5.724	5.468	5.229	5.008	4.802	4.611
15	7.191	6.811	6.462	6.142	5.847	5.575	5.324	5.092	4.876	4.675
16	7.379	6.974	6.604	6.265	5.954	5.668	5.405	5.162	4.938	4.730
17	7.549	7.120	6.729	6.373	6.047	5.749	5.475	5.222	4.990	4.775
18	7.702	7.250	6.840	6.467	6.128	5.818	5.534	5.273	5.033	4.812
19	7.839	7.366	6.938	6.550	6.198	5.877	5.584	5.316	5.070	4.843
20	7.963	7.469	7.025	6.623	6.259	5.929	5.628	5.353	5.101	4.870

FORMULAE

Valuation models

(i) Irredeemable preference share, paying a constant annual dividend, d, in perpetuity, where P_0 is the ex-div value:

$$P_0 = \frac{d}{k_{pref}}$$

(ii) Ordinary (equity) share, paying a constant annual dividend, d, in perpetuity, where P_0 is the ex-div value:

$$P_0 = \frac{d}{k_e}$$

(iii) Ordinary (equity) share, paying an annual dividend, d, growing in perpetuity at a constant rate, g, where P_0 is the ex-div value:

$$P_0 = \frac{d_1}{k_e - g} \quad \text{or} \quad P_0 = \frac{d_0[1+g]}{k_e - g}$$

(iv) Irredeemable (undated) debt, paying annual after-tax interest, $i[1-t]$, in perpetuity, where P_0 is the ex-interest value:

$$P_0 = \frac{i[1-t]}{k_{d\,net}}$$

or, without tax:

$$P_0 = \frac{i}{k_d}$$

(v) Total value of the geared firm, V_g (based on MM):

$$V_g = V_u + TB_c$$

(vi) Future value of S, of a sum X, invested for n periods, compounded at r% interest:

$$S = X[1+r]^n$$

(vii) Present value of 1·00 payable or receivable in n years, discounted at r% per annum:

$$PV = \frac{1}{[1+r]^n}$$

(viii) Present value of an annuity of 1·00 per annum, receivable or payable for n years, commencing in one year, discounted at r% per annum:

$$PV = \frac{1}{r}\left[1 - \frac{1}{[1+r]^n}\right]$$

(ix) Present value of 1·00 per annum, payable or receivable in perpetuity, commencing in one year, discounted at r% per annum:

$$PV = \frac{1}{r}$$

(x) Present value of 1·00 per annum, receivable or payable, commencing in one year, growing in perpetuity at a constant rate of g% per annum, discounted at r% per annum:

$$PV = \frac{1}{r-g}$$

Cost of capital

(i) Cost of irredeemable preference capital, paying an annual dividend, *d*, in perpetuity, and having a current ex-div price P_0:

$$k_{pref} = \frac{d}{P_0}$$

(ii) Cost of irredeemable debt capital, paying annual net interest, $i\,[1 - t]$, and having a current ex-interest price P_0:

$$k_{d\,\text{net}} = \frac{i[1 - t]}{P_0}$$

(iii) Cost of ordinary (equity) share capital, paying an annual dividend, *d*, in perpetuity, and having a current ex-div price P_0:

$$k_e = \frac{d}{P_0}$$

(iv) Cost of ordinary (equity) share capital, having a current ex-div price, P_0, having just paid a dividend, d_0, with the dividend growing in perpetuity by a constant g% per annum:

$$k_e = \frac{d_1}{P_0} + g \quad \text{or} \quad k_e = \frac{d_0[1 + g]}{P_0} + g$$

(v) Cost of ordinary (equity) share capital, using the CAPM:

$$k_e = R_f + [R_m - R_f]ß$$

(vi) Cost of ordinary (equity) share capital in a geared firm (no tax):

$$k_{eg} = k_o + [k_o - k_d]\,\frac{V_D}{V_E}$$

(vii) Cost of ordinary (equity) share capital in a geared firm (with tax):

$$k_{eg} = k_{eu} + [k_{eu} - k_d]\,\frac{V_D\,[1-t]}{V_E}$$

(viii) Weighted average cost of capital, k_0:

$$k_0 = k_{eg}\left[\frac{V_E}{V_E + V_D}\right] + k_d\left[\frac{V_D}{V_E + V_D}\right]$$

(ix) Adjusted cost of capital (MM formula):

$$K_{adj} = k_{eu}\,[1 - tL] \qquad \text{or} \qquad r^* = r[1 - T^*L]$$

In the following formulae, $ß_u$ is used for an ungeared ß and $ß_g$ is used for a geared ß:

(x) $ß_u$ from $ß_g$, taking $ß_d$ as zero (no tax):

$$ß_u = ß_g\left[\frac{V_E}{V_E + V_D}\right]$$

(xi) $ß_u$ from $ß_g$, taking $ß_d$ as zero (with tax):

$$ß_u = ß_g\left[\frac{V_E}{V_E + V_D\,[1-t]}\right]$$

Other formulae

(i) Interest rate parity (international Fisher effect):

$$\text{Forward rate US\$/£} = \text{Spot US\$/£} \times \frac{1+\text{nominal US interest rate}}{1+\text{nominal UK interest rate}}$$

(ii) Purchasing power parity (law of one price):

$$\text{Forward rate US\$/£} = \text{Spot US\$/£} \times \frac{1+\text{US inflation rate}}{1+\text{UK inflation rate}}$$

(iii) Link between nominal (money) and real interest rates:

[1 + nominal (money) rate] = [1 + real interest rate][1 + inflation rate]

(iv) Equivalent annual cost:

$$\text{Equivalent annual cost} = \frac{PV \text{ of costs over } n \text{ years}}{n \text{ year annuity factor}}$$

(v) Theoretical ex-rights price:

$$\text{TERP} = \frac{1}{N+1}[(N \times \text{cum rights price}) + \text{issue price}]$$

(vi) Value of a right:

$$\text{Value of a right} = \frac{\text{Rights on price} - \text{issue price}}{N+1}$$

or

$$\frac{\text{Theoretical ex rights price} - \text{issue price}}{N}$$

where N = number of rights required to buy one share.

The Examiner for FLFS offers to future candidates and to lecturers using this booklet for study purposes, the following background and guidance on the questions included in this examination paper.

Section A – compulsory

Question One concerns a UK-based computer technology business that has "re-privatised". The company trades worldwide, although its main market outside the UK is in North America. The company is evaluating the establishment of a new manufacturing, marketing and administration facility in either the UK or North America. Ideally, it would like to do both, but it does not have the financial and management resources to do so. The company has a policy of capital rationing, which involves limiting its capital investment in any one financial year to £50 million.

The company has already incurred some capital expenditure this year and, if it proceeds with one of the investment alternatives, the total capital expenditure for the year would exceed this capital limit. The question requires an evaluation of the two investments taking into account the different currencies involved and the appropriateness of limiting investment to £50 million in the current financial year. It further requires an analysis of the various types of risk involved in the two investments followed by a recommendation of whether the company should invest in either or both projects. The question tests learning outcomes in three syllabus sections: (i) *Formulation and achievement of financial objectives and strategy*; (iii) *Risk Management*; and (iv) *Advanced Investment Appraisal.*

Section B – two questions from four

Question Two concerns a manufacturer of pharmaceutical products based in the USA. The organisation exports worldwide and has a network of affiliates. At present, each affiliate has control over its own cash management and currency risk management decisions, but the organisation is considering centralising these functions. The question requires candidates to show the pattern of cash flows that would have been if such a system had been in operation. It also requires discussion of the characteristics of bi- and multi-lateral netting and of the advantages to the company from centralising its cash management and foreign exchange management policies. The question tests learning outcomes in syllabus sections (i) and (iii) *Risk Management.*

Question Three concerns two organisations that operate department stores in Europe. They have had similar earnings records over the past ten years and have similar capital structures. However, they have followed dissimilar dividend policies. The chairman of one of the organisations believes that his organisation's share price could have suffered because of its dividend policy. The question requires a discussion of the dividend policies followed by the two organisations and a general discussion of whether or not there is an optimal dividend policy that might affect shareholder value. It further examines the issue of share repurchase, how such a repurchase may be arranged, its purposes and the potential problems of such action. The question tests learning outcomes in syllabus sections (i) and (ii).

Question Four concerns an organisation based in Germany with a subsidiary in the UK. The organisation has borrowings in both Euros and Sterling; one of the loans is at a variable rate of interest and one at a fixed rate. The CEO of the organisation has asked a series of questions about the real costs of borrowing in these two currencies and what the opportunities are for borrowing in different currencies. Some discussion of methods for managing interest rate risk is also required. The question tests learning outcomes in syllabus section (iii).

Question Five concerns a medium-sized listed company based in the UK, which retails new and used motor cars. It also owns a substantial amount of land and property, much of which it rents or leases. The company has grown organically for the last few years, but is now considering expansion by acquisition. It has been approached by a smaller organisation that owns a franchise of a more expensive motor manufacturer. The bid would, therefore, be an agreed bid if terms can be negotiated to the satisfaction of both groups of shareholders. The question requires calculation of a range of valuations within which the bidder and target should negotiate, an assessment of the commercial and financial issues that might affect the bid; an evaluation of the most appropriate form of funding the bid given the current financial structures of the two companies and, finally, a discussion of the advantages and disadvantages of growth by acquisition as compared to growth by organic means. The question tests learning outcomes in two syllabus sections (i) and (ii).

CIMA

The Examiner's Answers for Management Accounting – Financial Strategy

SECTION A

Answer to Question One

Requirement (a)

Step 1
Calculate the asset beta, that is the beta of an ungeared firm, using the proxy company's beta. The estimated market value of RGB, using industry average P/E ratio is £800·28m (£76 million x 10·53).

ßu	=	ßg x 800/[800 + (320 x 1 - 0·3)]
	=	1·3 x (800/1024)
	=	1·016

Step 2
Calculate the discount rate using the CAPM

DR	=	Rf + ß (Rm - RF)
	=	5% + 1·016 (9% - 5%)
	=	9·06%, say 9% for evaluation purposes

Note: The book value proportions could be used but, according to theory, it is market values that are correct. If book value used, Bu is 0·84 and the discount rate would be 8·4%.

Limitations:

- The discount rate assumes that unsystematic risk has been diversified away. This is a private company with a small number of shareholders, so may be inappropriate.
- Assumes risk of investment same as company as a whole; in the UK this is new manufacturing plant not a new product, so the risk may be lower than the average.
- CAPM is a single period model and the risk may change over the life of the project, which here is 5 years. It also assumes that past variability with the market will continue.
- Use of proxy company's beta and industry P/E may be unreliable as businesses may not be the same and RGB may not be "average". Also, the post tax figures may be unreliable because of likely differences in the taxation situation of the two companies.

Requirement (b)

NPV calculations are below.

Profitability Index is calculated as (NPV + Initial Investment)/Initial investment

US Investment		*UK Investment*	
48·65/44·12 =	1·103	34·02/30 =	1·134

Accounting rate of return is calculated as average profits as a percentage of average investment:

	US Investment	*UK Investment*
Cum. Post-tax cash flows £m	67·78	42·88
Less: Depreciation £M	44·12	30·00
Profit	23·66	12·88
Average over 5 years	4·73	2·57
Average investment assuming straight line depreciation	22·06	15·00
ARR	21·44	17·13
	(4·73/22·06 x 100)	(2·57/15·00 x 100)

Exchange rates £1 =

Spot rate	1·7
1 year	1·683 $\left(\frac{1\cdot015}{1\cdot025}\right)$
2 years	1·667 ($1\cdot015^2/1\cdot025^2$)
3 years	1·651 ($1\cdot015^3/1\cdot025^3$)

Evaluation of US Investment

Year	*0*	*1*	*2*	*3*	*4*	*5*
US Investment						
Cash flow (US$)	-75·00	22·25	24·25	26·25		
Converted to £	-44·12	13·22	14·55	15·90	16·70	17·53
Tax @ 30%	13·24	-3·97	-4·36	-4·77	-5·01	-5·26
Payable		9·27	-4·36	-4·77	-5·01	-5·26
After-tax cash flows	-44·12	22·49	10·19	11·13	11·69	12·27
Discount Factor (DF) @ 5%	*1·000*	*0·952*	*0·907*	*0·864*	*0·823*	*0·784*
Certainty Equivalent (CE)	*1·000*	*0·900*	*0·870*	*0·820*	*0·700*	*0·700*
Adj. DR (DF x CE)	1	0·857	0·789	0·708	0·576	0·548
DCF £million	-44·12	19·27	8·04	7·88	6·73	6·73

NPV £million 4·53

Evaluation of UK Investment

Year	0	1	2	3	4	5
Cash flow (£million)	-30·00	6·30	9·00	10·50	11.03	11.58
Tax @ 30%	9·00	-1·89	-2·70	-3·15	-3.31	-3.47
Payable		7·11	-2·70	-3·15	-3.31	-3.47
After tax cash flows	-30·00	13·41	6·30	7·35	7·72	8·10
DF @ 9·06% Say 9%	1	0·917	0·842	0·772	0·708	0·650
DCF	-30·00	12·30	5·30	5·68	5·47	5·27

NPV £million 4·02

Requirement (c)

Report

To: Board of RGB

From: Capital Investment Analyst

Date: 23 November 2004

Subject: Investment in new facilities in USA or UK

(i) Introduction

You have asked me to evaluate the proposed investment in new manufacturing plant and associated facilities in either the USA or UK.

There are three main sections to this report.

- An evaluation of how the two investments will contribute to the achievement of the company's stated objectives.
- An analysis of the various types of risk involved in these investments and advice on a strategy for managing those risks.

The report concludes with a recommendation of a course of action.

(ii) An evaluation of how the two investments will contribute to the achievement of the company's stated objectives.

In summary, the results of the appraisal are as follows:

Summary

	US Investment	**UK Investment**
NPV (£million)	4·53	4·02
Profitability Index	1·103	1·134
RoCE (%)	21·44	17·17
Increase in EPS (pence) (over 5 year period)	19·7	10·7

Comments can be made broadly under the headings of the three company objectives, although there will be some overlap and common considerations.

Increase in EPS/NPV Considerations (1st objective)

- Using NPV analysis, the US investment would be selected as it increases shareholder wealth by the greatest amount.

- The UK investment together with investments already committed, do not use the full amount of capital available. If the UK investment is chosen then the surplus funds should be invested in another positive NPV project or returned to shareholders. Surplus cash could be invested *short term* in the money market, but this is not in the shareholders' best interests in the long term.

- Investment in the US project together with other investments already committed would involve capital expenditure of approximately £61 million. If the company's capital investment limit of £50 million is inflexible then this investment is ruled out without further consideration.

- In theory both investments should be undertaken, as they both have positive NPVs, with increased borrowings if necessary.

- Both investments will increase EPS over the five year period. Without information on the performance of existing operations it is difficult to calculate whether either investment will significantly affect the achievement of a 5% per annum increase. However, because of the 100% first year tax allowance on capital investment it is likely that both the US and UK investments will have an impact in the first year of operations. For example, if we assume no growth in existing operations, then the impact in years 1 and 2 will be:

Current EPS	*US investment*		*UK investment*	
	year 1	*year 2*	*year 1*	*year 2*
	63·3	74·7	63·3	69·5
EPS from Investment	11·4	1·1	6·2	0·3
Total	74·7	75·8	69·5	69·8
Increase %	18·0	1·5	9·8	0·4

Note: EPS from investment is cash flow for the year less annual depreciation (capital investment/5) divided by shares in issue (120 million)

Accounting rate of return considerations (2nd objective)

- An accounting rate of return (RoCE here) attempts to measure profit and capital cost on the same basis as adopted in preparing accounts. The method can be based on average investment or on initial investment method. Here, as a simplification, we have taken average annual profits as a percentage of average investment over the five-year period.

- It has the advantage of simplicity and is readily understood by non-finance managers, but it does not take into account timing or variations in cash flows, projects with different lives and risks and so on.

- It should not be used for resource allocation, which should use cash flows rather than profit.

- Here there is a RoCE, or accounting rate of return of over 20% for the US investment, but below 20% for the UK investment. The two measures, RoSF and RoCE are not identical, but assuming it is shareholders who require the highest return (compared with debt) and the investment is funded with equity, then RoCE is an acceptable proxy. Last year, the company failed to meet this objective and showed a RoSF of little over 18% (earnings of £76 million/shareholders' funds of £420 million).

Maintaining a global presence (3rd objective)

- If the company wishes to maintain a global presence in its operating markets, then it needs to maintain an adequate investment programme. Investment in the US would probably contribute more to "global" presence, which may justify choosing this project, even though it means increased borrowing.

- However, meeting this objective implies the company should be looking to invest in projects outside the US and UK, so neither investment would contribute much.

Summary

- As can be seen from the comparison of these two investments – NPV and RoCE and increase in EPS all suggest the US investment should be chosen. Only the PI criterion suggests the UK investment. When capital is rationed, as here, and a choice has to be made, then PI should be considered along with NPV, but managers may be rewarded on accounting measures such as RoCE and EPS.

(ii) *An analysis of the various types of risk involved in these investments and advice on a strategy for managing those risks.*

The four main areas of risk that can be discussed are: economic, commercial, political and technical.

Economic risk

- Inflation forecast suggests the US$ will strengthen against the £, but this could change. The risk could be hedged using external methods such as forward markets or possibly financing with a $ loan. Internal methods such as netting and matching may be better here as RGB has substantial operations in the US already.
- There is no interest rate risk as a *direct* consequence of these investments so hedging this type of risk not entirely relevant.
- The CAPM has been used to determine a discount rate for the UK investment using a proxy company's beta. The company may not be so similar to RGB that this beta is appropriate. Sensitivity analysis could be used to help evaluate the investment's sensitivity to the rate.
- The certainty equivalents used for the US investment are inevitably subjective. Again, sensitivity analysis could be used.

Commercial/technical risk

- The investments appear to be in mainstream businesses and do not involve new product development so do not appear excessively risky.
- As much of the company's business is in the USA there may be advantages in setting up a manufacturing base close to customers in the US. This would minimise some of the commercial risks associated with the US investment.

Political risk

- Political risk is not a major issue here other than potential changes to tax regime, eg extension of unitary taxation system.

(iii) *Recommendation and conclusion*

- Both investments would increase EPS over a five-year period, and both have positive NPVs at the chosen discount rate. The US investment would increase EPS and shareholder wealth by a greater amount than the UK investment. The discount rate in the US investment may be overly pessimistic; there is relatively low business risk, virtually no political risk and the foreign currency risk could be managed by a combination of external and internal hedging techniques, given RGB already has substantial investments in the US.

- The US investment meets the RoCE criteria whereas the UK investment does not, but this is not an appropriate measure on which to base investment decisions.

- The US investment would probably contribute to "global presence" more than the UK investment, but an investment in a third country might be more appropriate for this objective.
- If the capital expenditure limit is absolute, then the UK investment must be chosen but my recommendations are:

  (i) If the choice is between only these two investments, then choose the US investment and break the capital expenditure limit, even if this means borrowing an extra £11 million. This extra borrowing would have a marginal effect on the company's gearing and WACC;

  (ii) Consider alternative investments that might contribute more to the company's third objective.

SECTION B

Answer to Question Two

Requirement (a)

- Payments go back and forwards between affiliates, but only net amount transferred to Group HQ;
- An example using a bi-lateral arrangement between two affiliates in two different countries: Affiliate A sells goods worth US$1million to Affiliate B, which, in turn, sells goods worth US$2 million to Affiliate A. The combined flows total US$3 million. Using a netting system Affiliate A pays Affiliate B US$1 million. Bi-lateral netting may not involve a central treasury department;
- With numerous affiliates, the system becomes more complex but provides more opportunity for cost saving, for example more efficient use of staff resources;
- Essential to a multi-lateral netting scheme is a control point or netting centre, usually sited in the central treasury department, which will use a matrix as shown below;
- All payables and receivables need to be stated in a common currency. On an inter-company or group basis the payables will always equal the receivables;
- Funds payable to, or receivable from, external organisations could be brought into the scheme to reduce group costs even further, but increases complexity;
- The impact of currency changes on the amounts scheduled for transfer would be minimised by fixing the exchange rate at which the transactions occur.

In the example here, there would be 11 separate payments being made. Multi-lateral netting would have reduced the amounts of these transfers to US$24 million and the number of payments to three.

Inter–Companies Payments Matrix (US$ Millions)

Receiving Affiliate	*Paying Affiliate* French	British	Italian	Canadian	*Total Receipts*	*Net Receipt (Payment)*
French	–	16	14	8	38	20 (38 - 18)
British	12	–	8	4	24	4 (24 - 20)
Italian	4	0	–	6	10	-22 (10 - 32)
Canadian	2	4	10	–	16	-2 (16 - 18)
Total Payments	18	20	32	18	88	0

The inter company transfers will be as follows:

	$million
The Italian affiliate pays the French affiliate	20
The Italian affiliate pays the British affiliate	2
The Canadian affiliate pays the British affiliate	2
	24

This can be shown diagrammatically as below.

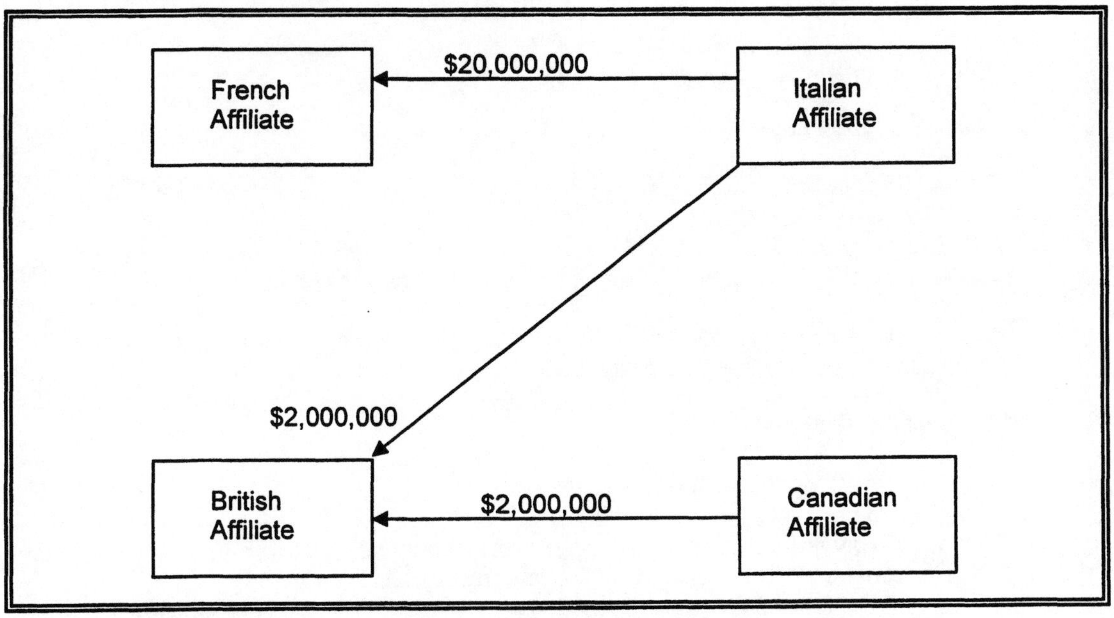

How the Italian affiliate pays $22 million is beyond the scope of this question.

Note: Alternative sets of multilateral payments are possible. The choice of which affiliate each payer pays depends on the relative costs of transferring funds between each pair of affiliates and also if funds from third parties are brought into the scheme.

Requirement (b)

There are common benefits and disadvantages of centralised cash and foreign currency management, although they are separate issues. Centralised cash management concerns the pooling of inter-company balances once converted to a common currency, in the example here it is the US$.

Centralised forex management relates primarily to the management of risk and decisions on hedging techniques, before the cash balances are remitted.

The benefits are:

Centralised cash management:

- Better interest rates might be obtained for larger amounts, especially if they are planned in advance;
- Possibly lower transaction costs, bank commissions etc;
- More control for the parent, more visibility of cash resources;
- Possibly better management of cash resources;

Centralised forex management

- Takes control of risk and determination of risk management, for example choice of hedging policy;
- Combined with centralised cash management, this would allow access to more internal hedging techniques, as demonstrated in part (a) of this question. For example, if a subsidiary in France owes a supplier in the UK £s, at present the subsidiary might hedge using forward markets. With a centralised system, the parent might be able to net off the amount owed in the UK with similar amounts due from a customer in the UK

to another subsidiary – not necessarily in France. This would almost certainly be cheaper although administratively more complex.

Disadvantages:

Centralised cash management

- Possibly higher transaction costs;
- Administrative complexities might make such a system difficult to operate effectively in practice, for example obtaining cash transfers in a timely manner;
- A system would need to be in place to allow subsidiaries to obtain funds quickly should an unexpected, justifiable demand arise.

Centralised forex management

- Costs of converting money back and forward;
- Risk of unexpected changes in exchange rates cannot be dealt with as easily (although this is doubtful if we are dealing with major currencies.)

From the parent's point of view the main benefit may be in control and reduced costs overall. From the subsidiaries' viewpoint, they lose the flexibility of short-term investment and are constantly under the scrutiny of head office.

The choice depends on the company's objectives and strategy towards cash and foreign currency management policies and management of its subsidiaries.

Answer to Question Three

Requirement (a)

(i) **Dividend policies and effect on market value**

Payout and P/E ratios for the two companies are as follows:

	AB		*YZ*	
	Payout	*P/E*	*Payout*	*P/E*
1999	26	9·1	40	9·2
2000	40	10·0	40	10·6
2001	60	10·0	40	15·6
2002	–	–	–	–
2003	60	10·0	40	13·9
2004	40	9·3	40	11·7

- Investors usually expect a constant dividend policy and a large rise or fall in any one year can have a significant effect on a company's share price.
- Both companies have had constant policies, which act as a signal to investors:

  AB has followed a policy of paying a fixed amount of 60 cents per share each year, including 2002 when the company sustained a loss. As earnings were actually declining, this meant a decreasing amount available for investment. The unwillingness of the company to restrict dividends when the company's earnings were underperforming is likely to have led to continued low growth and a negative effect on share price and market value.

YZ has paid a fixed payout ratio of 40% of earnings each year, excluding 2002 when this company also sustained a loss. This meant that shareholders received widely varying dividends from 0 in 2002, 36 cents in years 2001 and 2003 and 96 cents in 1999. This may seem logical, but unless the market and shareholders are fully aware of this potential volatility it may result in sending negative signals to the market. However it increases share price volatility. In 2002, when the profits of both companies fell, AB's shares fell by 20% whereas YZ's fell by 35%.

- There is no definite relationship between the share price and dividend policy of these two companies. If AB continued to pay dividends when it was loss-making on the basis of sending signals to the market, this had little effect as the market value and P/E ratio were lower than YZ, which had similar losses.

- YZ had a rights issue in 2003 when shares were apparently at a low ebb following a year of losses. This might not have been a sensible time to launch a rights issue, but may have been necessary as a survival tactic. Compared to AB, it does not seem to have had too adverse an effect on share price.

- In 1999, the two companies had similar EPS and P/E ratios, but AB having more shares in issue had a higher market value. Since 1999 YZ has been given a higher growth rating by the market, as evidenced by the P/E ratio. This might suggest the market prefers a dividend policy of a constant payout ratio, but this is unlikely. The market is more likely to be reacting to YZ's business strategy.

- In practice there is unlikely to be a single "optimal" dividend policy for all investors as some will prefer dividends and some capital growth. Evidence is sparse that the "clientele" effect has a strong influence on investor preferences in any given company.

(ii) **Optimal dividend policy**

In theory, according to Modigliani and Miller, dividend payments are irrelevant to the value of the firm. However, this theory makes three basic assumptions:

1 Perfect capital markets, no tax differentials and no transaction costs

2 Rational investors, indifferent to return as capital gain or dividend

3 Certainty about the future investment programme

These assumptions may be considered unrealistic, although probably not so unrealistic as to void the theory altogether. Capital markets are fairly efficient, at least for the larger companies' shares, there are few tax differentials that really matter and transaction costs are relatively insignificant especially for the larger investors.

It is unlikely there is an "optimal" dividend policy for any firm as noted above. In theory, if a company has sufficient positive NPV investment, it should pay 0 in dividends; if it has no such investments it should return 100% of earnings to shareholders as dividends. Companies rarely do this. In a listed company, the "signalling" mechanism of dividends is believed to have a strong influence on company directors who insist on paying maintained or even increased dividends when they should be reducing them, as evidenced by AB maintaining its dividend in the face of falling earnings and even losses. This policy does not seem to have translated into higher share price performance.

Requirement (b)

Methods of share repurchase
Shares may be repurchased by one of the following methods:

- purchase on the open market;
- individual arrangement with institutional investors;
- a tender offer to all shareholders.

An individual arrangement with institutional investors tends to be the most popular approach as it is the quickest, most efficient means of returning surplus cash. Often, therefore, only a small group of shareholders will participate in a share repurchase, whereas all shareholders will participate in a special dividend. A further consideration in the return of surplus cash concerns the possible tax implications for investors. A share repurchase may lead to a capital gains tax liability for participating investors, while a special dividend would normally attract an income tax liability.

Reasons for share repurchase
The repurchase of a company's shares may be carried out for a number of reasons:

- return of surplus cash to investors;
- to reduce the company's cost of capital;
- to enhance earnings per share in the hope of also increasing market price per share;
- to prevent, or reduce the likelihood of, unwelcome takeover bids;
- to adjust the gearing of the company to a higher level, closer to the company's optimal capital structure;
- to reduce the amount of cash needed to pay future dividends.

Potential problems of share repurchase are:

- It may suggest a failure of management to identify projects that will generate returns above the company's cost of capital. However, the logic is that returning capital to shareholders gives the shareholders the opportunity to generate higher returns for themselves by investing elsewhere;
- If the arrangement is with institutional investors, subject to shareholder agreement, not all shareholders will be able to participate;
- Determining a price that is fair to all can be difficult;
- Tax disadvantages, for example shareholders may become liable for capital gains tax at an inconvenient time.

The majority of share repurchases, and special dividends are the result of companies having surplus cash in excess of their operational requirements, for example Vodafone in the UK.

An example of dividend versus repurchase
AB has excess cash of €2·5 million (or 10 cents per share) and is considering payment of this amount as an extra dividend. The Chairman has forecast that earnings will be €40 million next year, or €1·60 for each of the 25 million shares outstanding. The price earnings ratio is 9·3, so the shares of the firm should sell for €14·88.

Alternatively, AB could use the excess cash to repurchase some of its own stock. Assume a tender offer of €15 a share is made. Here 166,667 shares will be repurchased so that the total number of shares remaining is 24·83 million. With fewer shares outstanding, the earnings per share will rise from 160 cents to 161·1 cents. The price-earning ratio remains at 9·3, since both the business and financial risks of the firm are the same in the repurchase case as they were for the dividend case. Thus the price of a share after the repurchase is €14·98.

If commissions, taxes and other imperfections are ignored, the stockholders should be indifferent between a dividend and a repurchase. With dividends, each stockholder owns a share worth €14·88 and receives 10 cents in dividends, so that the total value is €14·98.

This example illustrates that, in a perfect market, the firm is indifferent between a dividend payment and a share repurchase. This is similar to the indifference propositions established by MM. The calculations here make a number of assumptions and only a small number of shares are redeemed, so the effect is minimal. However, the principle is confirmed that share repurchase leads to an increase of 10 cents in share price, all other things being equal.

However, the financial press may place undue emphasis on EPS figures in a repurchase agreement. Given the irrelevance propositions of MM, an increase in EPS need not be beneficial. When a repurchase is financed by excess cash, in a perfect capital market the total value to the stockholder should remain the same under the dividend payment strategy as under the repurchase agreement strategy.

Answer to Question Four

Memorandum

To: Chief Executive

From: Assistant Treasurer

Date: 23 November 2004

Subject: Interest rate and foreign exchange rate risk management policies

I refer to your recent request to provide information on the potential for profiting from foreign exchange rate differentials. First of all, it might be useful to explain the main underlying theories about the relationship between interest rates, exchange rates and inflation. One of my key roles as Assistant Treasurer is to evaluate different financing strategies given the imperfections and inefficiencies that can exist in financial markets.

Purchasing power parity
This theory suggests that if the rate of inflation in one country is greater than the rate of inflation in another country, exchange rates will adjust to offset the differential, therefore the cost of living in each country would be the same. Put another way, the expected difference in inflation rates between two countries equals, in equilibrium, the expected movement in spot rates.

Interest rate parity
Interest rates are determined in the market by supply and demand (although we should note political interference). There is a relationship between foreign exchange and money markets. Other things being equal, the currency with the higher interest rate will sell at a discount in the forward market against the currency with the lower interest rate. This is because higher interest rates imply higher inflation, which is a negative indicator of economic strength.

I now respond to your specific points.

1 *The real rate of interest is calculated as follows:*

[1 + nominal rate = (1 + real rate) (1 + expected rate of inflation)] - 1

For our sterling loan this is

1·08 = (1 + x) (1 + 0·025) - 1 = 0·0536 or 5·4%

For our ECCA loan this is:

1·06 = (1 + x) (1 + 0·015) - 1 = 0·0443 or 4·4%

2 *Borrowing in Euros, Sterling or US$*

Ideally, the currency of the loan should be matched with the currency of the assets financed. This will provide a natural hedge against exchange rate volatility. Although this will reduce exchange rate risk on the loan, GH may incur higher costs by borrowing in a currency that moves adversely against the Euro. In this case, based on the base rates and forecast inflation rates, the Euro is expected to weaken against the US$, but strengthen against sterling. GH does, of course, have a sterling-denominated asset – its UK subsidiary.

If sterling weakens against the Euro, GH will pay a lower real rate of interest by borrowing in Euros rather than sterling. Over time the process of arbitrage should ensure that real rates equalise in the UK, the Euro zone and the USA.

A further factor to consider is that GH currently pays a higher premium over base rate in its Sterling loan than its Euro loan.

A Eurobond is a bearer bond, issued in a euro currency, usually Euro dollars, which are US dollars deposited with, or borrowed from, a bank outside the US. They are not Euro-denominated bonds. A key advantage of the Eurobond market is that it allows for a greater range of potential investors. From the investor's point of view, the bearer bond format may be attractive, although this raises considerations for the safe keeping of the documents. Other benefits from the company's point of view are as follows:

- They are usually cheaper than equivalent domestic bonds;
- The market is more flexible, allowing tailor-made financial instruments;
- They may provide a hedge against interest rate or currency movements;
- The cost of the issue may be lower than the US corporate bond market.

3 *Interest rate risk management*

Interest-rate risk management requires a company treasurer to use techniques to reduce the risk to his company caused by its vulnerability to changes in interest rates and the need to pay higher returns to lenders. There are other risks – such as the possibility of rates increasing shortly before the launch of new capital – but these are a matter for good judgement rather than risk management issues.

Here, the Euro denominated loan has a fixed interest rate and the risk is that if interest rates fall, competitors with loans at a floating rate may gain an advantage. One way to manage this type of risk is to use an interest rate swap. The key features are:

- The ability to obtain finance, or cheaper finance than by borrowing directly in the market, if one company has a comparative advantage in terms of credit rating. This provides an arbitrage opportunity which can be shared by the participants to the swap.
- Interest-rate commitments can be altered without redeeming old debt or issuing new debt, which is an expensive procedure.

- Swaps can be developed to meet specific needs, and there are many innovative products on the markets – for example, zero-coupon swaps, or "swaptions".

The sterling loan is at a variable rate, which brings the risk that interest costs increase thus reducing profits. Forward rate agreements (FRAs) may be used to minimise this risk. FRAs are agreements between a company and a bank that fixes the rate of interest for borrowing at a certain time in the future. If the interest rate is higher than the agreed rate, the bank pays the difference.

Interest-rate futures and options could also be used. Interest rate futures are traded forms of FRAs. They are for standard amounts and maturity dates. With an interest rate option an organisation can arrange, for example, for a bank to purchase, lend or borrow at a guaranteed interest rate at some specified future time. A premium would be payable for this. If interest rates have moved in the company's favour by the "specified future time", the organisation can allow the option to lapse.

4 *Hedging of loan interest payments*

If we were to pay our loan interest today, we would pay £10 million x 8% = £800,000 at current exchange rate this is £800,000 x 1·81 = €1,448,000.

If we use interest rate parity, as explained above, we can use the following formula to forecast forward rates as long as we know the spot rate and expected annual interest rates.

$$\text{Forward rate Euro/£} = \text{Spot Euro/£} \times \frac{1+\text{nominal Euro interest rate}}{1+\text{UK nominal interest rate}}$$

In the example here, the figures are:

$$\text{Forward rate Euro/£} = 1\cdot81 * \frac{\sqrt{1+0\cdot035}}{\sqrt{1+0\cdot050}} = 1\cdot7970$$

The central banks' base rates given in the question are annual rates. Therefore, forward rates for 6 months' time are calculated using the square root of (1 + the published annual rate).

> **Examiner's Note:**
> Simply dividing the annual rate by 2 is not strictly correct, but would be an acceptable simplification in an examination.

The calculation shows an appreciation in the exchange rate for the Euro against Sterling over the six-month period. If we use the rate of 1·7970 we can expect to pay loan interest of:

£800,000 x 1·7970 = €1,437,600

We could also use purchasing power parity and forecast rates of inflation to arrive at a forward rate. In theory, we should arrive at the same rate although slight imperfections in the market may cause minor distortions.

To demonstrate, I replace interest rates with inflation rates and use the same formula given above.

$$\text{Forward rate Euro/£} = 1\cdot81 * \frac{\sqrt{1+0\cdot015}}{\sqrt{1+0\cdot025}} = 1\cdot8012$$

I use the square root of 1 + the annual inflation rate to arrive at a six-month rate. The Euro is still likely to appreciate against Sterling, although at a slightly lower rate than when we used interest rate parity. However inflation forecasts are rather less precise and reliable than interest rates, in advanced countries at least.

If we use this forward rate, the interest payment expected would be:

£800,000 x 1·8012 = €1,440,960.

These calculations mean that as the Euro is expected to appreciate against Sterling, we are likely to pay less interest in Euros in 6 months' time than we would if we had to pay that interest today. Hedging is a risk reduction technique and if this was a "one-off" payment and we had no business operations in the UK we might well be advised to take out a forward market contract to lock in our position. Of course, if the Euro appreciates more than the market expects we would forgo a windfall profit.

However, there are two factors that suggest hedging using a forward contract is not appropriate in the situation we have here. These are:

1 We make interest payments every six months and we need to look further ahead than the next payment. Forward contracts are usually for a maximum of twelve months, although it is possible to make special arrangements, at a cost.

2 We have extensive business operations in the UK. In our circumstances we have no real need to hedge using external markets as we have Sterling revenue streams that we could net off against the interest payment. If, for internal reasons, we do not want to do this, we could ask our bank to help us arrange a swap.

5 *Fixed versus floating rate borrowing*

Fixed rate finance may be preferred because interest payment commitments are known. This type of finance will be especially useful if interest rates are expected to rise. Floating rate finance would be preferred if interest rates are expected to fall, or if the company has floating assets which will provide a better match, for example debtors.

Currently GH has a balance of fixed and floating rate debt. Interest rates are currently low, which provides an argument for taking out fixed rate loans for longer term periods. However, if the markets are efficient this will have already been factored into quoted interest rates.

If interest rates are expected to increase in the foreseeable future, GH is not over exposed to higher rates as it has a fair amount of fixed loans in its balance sheet.

A further factor to consider is the currency of the loan. If sterling enters the Euro zone over the next few years, there will be a convergence between sterling rates and Euro zone rates. This is likely to result in a reduction in UK interest rates, and may therefore favour obtaining variable rates on sterling denominated loans.

Answer to Question Five

Part (i)

The price to be offered
Preliminary calculations
Note: Valuations for BST are provided here as well as for SM as BST's share values may be needed for the bid terms.

	BST Motors	*SM Limited*
Information in question (shown here in italics for convenience)		
EPS – pence	*112·5*	*153·0*
DPS – pence	*50·6*	*100·0*
Share price – pence	*1237*	*n/a*
No of shares (Million)	*25*	*1·5*

Three types of valuation are attempted here: market value, asset value and value based on the dividend valuation model. Capitalisation of earnings would also be an acceptable method. Brief comments on the method of valuation accompany the calculations.

Share price and market value using quoted share prices
Assuming market capitalisation is assumed to represent market value, current market value is derived from a combination of historic earnings, the market's expectations of future earnings and risk characteristics of the company. However, market prices may contain elements of speculative premium, particularly in a bid situation. The advantages are that, with a listed company, it is publicly available information and provides a benchmark for valuation. SM shares are not quoted, so the company does not have a market capitalisation, but clearly it has a value. We could use a "proxy" P/E ratio if one were available, for example the industry average. If we use BST's P/E – which may or may not be at all representative – and apply it to SM's earnings, we get a value of £25·24 million (153 EPS x 11 P/E x 1·5 million shares in issue). Using forecast future earnings of £4 million we get a potential value of £44 million.

BST's P/E could be adjusted to take account of SM being unlisted and a smaller company, but it is debateable whether the adjustment should be up or down.

Share price and market value using Dividend Valuation Model

Po = D1/(Ke - g)

= 105/(0·10 - 0·05)

= **2100p**

Total equity value – £million = £21 x 1·5 million = **31·50**

This method of valuation requires knowledge of the cost of equity, dividend policy and the investment programme of the firm and assumes no external funding. In its simplest form it assumes constant growth although it can be adapted for other growth patterns. It assumes a share price is a function entirely of dividend policy and as such has serious limitations except as a benchmark. Here, we have assumed the dividend will be maintained at 100p plus 5% growth next year. Given that earnings are forecast to increase by 74% this may be too low. However, this forecast has been made by SM's Managing Director who clearly has an interest in showing the company's financial prospects in the most favourable light. An increase of 74% seems extremely high and warrants some scepticism. As this will be an agreed bid if it proceeds, BST should be able to verify the forecast.

Clearly the difficulties faced by an outsider wishing to arrive at a valuation on the DVM basis are formidable. As in the question here, the difficulties are often suppressed by assuming that the future is a projection from the past. As BST is likely to gain access to SM's projections, as noted above, using the DVM with estimated figures for growth is unlikely to be necessary.

Asset-based value

Pence per share	45/1·5	=	**3000**

The expression "asset value" is largely restricted to tangible assets and is usually based on costs not values. Frequently it has little relevance except in specific circumstances such as a liquidation or disposal of parts of a business. However, the circumstances here are unusual in that BST appears to be as much a property company as a motor trader (similar situation to Woolworths in the UK). SM also appears to have substantial property assets. It also has a valuable franchise, which will not be reflected in the balance sheet. Details of this franchise need to be known before a true valuation can be obtained.

Price Range	*£m*	*Per share (pence)*
Market price	25/44	1667/2933 (current/forecast)
DVM	32	2100
Asset value	45	3000

Part (ii) **Financial factors that might affect the bid**

- As both P/E and DVM based valuations are below asset value, it is unlikely SM would consider an offer on these bases. Also, both use subjective estimates, which are unlikely to be anywhere near accurate.

- It is not clear how much cash BST has available. A share for share exchange will take longer to arrange and be more costly.

- The main business consideration is whether BST would want to be bothered with a deal of this relatively small size unless it was an entry vehicle into the prestige end of the motor distribution market. It is not clear from the question details that BST has any intention of diversifying into this "top end" market of which it has no experience. This suggests that part of the deal might involve retaining some of SM's management and employees.

- BST appears to be valued by the market at below asset value. This suggests either the assets are considered over valued in the balance sheet (unlikely) or the company, being relatively small, has avoided the scrutiny of the market. If BST does embark on a takeover, even an agreed one, it will arouse interest in the market and this discrepancy between asset value and market value would become subject to publicity. It could itself become a takeover target.

- SM is paying 65% of its earnings in dividends – not unusual for a small private company. If the dividend payout was reduced the valuation of the company might increase as funds could be retained for profitable investment (dividend irrelevancy theory notwithstanding).

- As SM has approached BST there is no reason why BST cannot get access to SM's forecasts and business strategy to determine a more accurate price.

- Will all SM's shareholders be agreeable to the bid, or could a sizeable minority frustrate negotiations.

- Are there any other interested buyers that could lead to a price war? Has BST looked at other investment/takeover opportunities?

Part (iii) **Funding the bid**

There are two methods to consider, cash and shares.

The asset value would appear to be the starting price. £45 million is a relatively small sum of money and BST would almost certainly pay cash, even if this means increasing borrowings. Its borrowings at present are around £77 million, assuming its debt is quoted at par.

Calculated as:

Debt ratio =	Debt/Market value of company =	20%
Debt therefore =	25% x (12·37 x 25 million) =	£77·3 million

If a further £45 million were to be raised, this would increase the debt ratio to 28%, [122·3/(309·25 + 122·3)] which is not excessive for a company with substantial asset value.

A share exchange would be more expensive and time consuming and would raise issues of dilution of EPS and control – how important this last issue might be is difficult to judge on the limited information available. However, it would have a favourable impact on the debt ratio, which would reduce to approximately 18% (£77 million/(£309 + 45 + 77).

If 100% of SM's shareholders were willing to accept shares, this would imply a minimum of 3·64 million new BST shares would have to be issued, assuming the current share price used as an exchange factor (£45 million/12·37). This is a ratio of 2·4 BST shares for each SM share. A combination of cash and shares is more likely to be the preferred option for most shareholders so BST needs to be prepared to negotiate.

Part (iv) **Organic growth versus acquisition**

Advantages of acquisition in general are often claimed as:

- Buys out or reduces competition – not relevant here.
- Allows increase in market size and therefore influence on the market to be achieved more quickly – possibly a factor here given the franchise and location issues.
- Potential for economies of scale and synergies – although often these fail to materialise and unlikely to be of great significance here.
- Unless the two companies' cash flows are perfectly positively correlated – unlikely – there will be some diversification of risk which might allow a lower cost of capital and hence increase in market value (all other things remaining equal).
- An advantage of an agreed bid is that there should be opportunities for sharing information to allow a realistic valuation and assessment of likely acquisition benefits. It is, therefore, likely to be faster than organic growth without the disadvantages of the unknown factors present in hostile bids.

Disadvantages are:

- Integration of businesses and company cultures can take longer, be more costly and difficult than anticipated.
- The amount of information on the target in an acquisition may be limited and leads to post-acquisition surprises.

CIMA

November 2004 Examinations

Final Level

Management Accounting – Information Strategy

(FLIS – Paper 14)

The answers published here have been written by the Examiner and should provide a helpful guide for both lecturers and students.

Published separately on the CIMA website (www.cimaglobal.com/students) from the end of March 2005 is a Post Examination Guide for this paper, which provides much valuable and complementary material including indicative mark information.

CIMA

Final Level

Management Accounting – Information Strategy

14

FLIS

25 November 2004

Thursday morning

INSTRUCTIONS TO CANDIDATES

Read this page before you look at the questions

You are allowed three hours to answer this question paper.
Answer the ONE question in Section A. Answer TWO questions ONLY from Section B.

SECTION A – 50 MARKS

ANSWER THIS QUESTION

Question One

Company overview

The JA Company (JA) manufactures large containers known as vats, and stirrers used in the mixing of various liquids including chemicals and dairy products. Vats vary in size from 1 metre in height with a 1 metre diameter to 15 metres in height with a diameter of around 8 metres. The vats are manufactured from a variety of materials including sheet metal, rubber and high quality plastics. Each vat is made to specific customer order and JA manufactures around 650 vats each year.

Purchasing and production systems

As each vat is made to order, purchasing and production do not take place until the order is confirmed. Customer information is maintained on a Customer Relationship Management (CRM) system, which also tracks the progress of each order. Sales representatives in JA maintain the CRM. They are also responsible for contact with customers, initial pricing of each order, and informing customers of the progress of each order through the production system.

When an order is confirmed, an email with the order details is sent to the Central Purchasing Department (CPD). The routing for the email is via an external Internet Service Provider as the CRM and CPD systems are maintained on separate servers and JA does not, at present, maintain a Local Area Network (LAN). At this stage, the CPD checks availability of materials to make the vat with JA Company stores and then with suppliers for any materials not currently in stock. The necessary materials are then ordered and a detailed costing for each individual vat produced.

When all the necessary materials to manufacture a vat are available, the manufacturing process commences. Manufacture is carried out by a CAD / CAM system, which sends information to the CRM.

When manufacture is complete, the vat is delivered to the customer. An email is sent from the CRM system, confirming despatch, to the accounts department. This acts as a trigger to commence the invoicing process.

The directors recognise that there are some deficiencies in this system, and hope to revise it in the near future.

Executive Information System (EIS)

The EIS relies mainly on the CRM for details of orders, production and sale of vats. The directors realise this is not ideal and a budget has already been approved to provide a new EIS which will be linked to the other operational systems in the company. An example of the output from the current EIS is shown below:

Contract number	*Cost £*	*Stage of production*	*Delivery date*
10761	10,000	Q	23.11.04
11094	23,060	M	11.11.04
2367a	49,362	M	12.12.04
0924	101,026	Q	15.01.05
10762	47,006	D	08.03.05
30608	43,226	D	02.04.05
89696	39,000	Q	25.01.05

The EIS was written 8 years ago by JA's IT department. However, since then, the department has been reduced in size and its function is now limited to enforcing company hardware and software standards, with all applications being purchased "off the shelf". Given the lack of knowledge in-house, the directors are considering different methods of producing a new EIS.

Another company, MDD, has already been contacted. MDD has suggested that the most cost-effective approach would be to use off-the-shelf software with minimal amendments to JA's specific systems. The managing director is inclined to agree with this view.

Other issues

Overall, staff in JA understand the weaknesses in the current Transaction Processing Systems (TPS) and EIS, and are realistic regarding what is currently available on the market for those systems. Staff have been particularly concerned with the delays in processing resulting from inadequate hardware and a centralised system.

MDD has also been asked to advise on the necessity for system change for the TPS. Initial indications are that an off-the-shelf system will be recommended. Staff will be involved in system design just prior to implementation to ensure that work practices can be amended to complement the new system.

Required:

(a) Explain the characteristics of information expected from an EIS, evaluating whether the information available from JA's current EIS satisfies those characteristics.

(12 marks)

(b) Using appropriate sections of the value chain as a framework for your answer, discuss the weaknesses of the current information systems in JA.

(15 marks)

(c) Evaluate whether outsourcing the development of the new EIS is appropriate for JA.

(12 marks)

(d) Discuss whether staff are likely to accept the changes to work practices likely to be brought about by new TPS and EIS.

(11 marks)

(Total = 50 marks)

End of Section A

SECTION B – 50 MARKS

ANSWER TWO QUESTIONS ONLY

Question Two

The NLE organisation sells a range of leisure products on the Internet including books, CDs, DVDs and computer games. The organisation's mission statement is *to be the most reliable and cost efficient supplier of books and CDs on the Internet.* It was formed six years ago, and has grown quickly. Two years ago it became one of the first Internet companies to report a net operating profit. NLE is recognised as being one of the market leaders on the Internet, and its share price is increasing at 20% per annum. In a recent market survey, 80% of people between the ages of 20 and 45 identified the NLE brand name as one they would use when ordering goods from the Internet.

The company now has a positive cash flow, with no outstanding loans. The directors are investigating alternative investments. One possibility is the purchase of 25 bookshops located in major cities in one country. These shops would be re-branded with the NLE name, and offer a similar range of products to the NLE Internet site. However, as no shop could hold the 2.5 million items currently available on the NLE site, a next-day "collect from shop" option would be made available. This means that customers could order goods from the Internet, or by visiting an NLE bookshop and then collect those goods on the next working day. Goods would be despatched overnight from NLE's main warehouse to fulfil these orders.

Required:

(a) Assuming that the Board of NLE decides to purchase the bookshops, advise them on the Information Strategy issues that they should consider, clearly explaining the information required when considering each issue.

NOTE: You are not required to advise on alternative sources of finance.

(15 marks)

(b) Identify and explain **two** Critical Success Factors and their supporting Performance Indicators that can be used to determine the success or otherwise of the purchase of the bookshops, should this acquisition go ahead.

(10 marks)

(Total = 25 marks)

Question Three

TT sells computer games on the Internet. The organisation has been trading for four years and has a customer base in excess of 700,000 names and addresses located in 10 different countries. Sales are made via an Internet site or by telephone ordering, with orders being taken by customer service staff. The ordering process is hindered slightly by lack of real-time integration between the stock and sales system on TT's computer systems.

Customer information is recorded within the sales ledger itself, making access and analysis difficult. The sales ledger database does not include the necessary relational features to enable full analysis of customer history information or to identify overall trends in purchases.

Now that the organisation is more financially secure, the directors have decided to implement a new sales ledger system, which will include a more detailed customer database. Features available in the database in addition to "normal" recording of sales invoices will include order history, unfilled order details, delivery time, customer payment options and total sales analysis by product, customer and country. This information will now be directly accessible by customer service representatives, rather than through the production of special reports on customer accounts by the new sales ledger system. The system will also interface directly with the stock management software providing some time savings in terms of input of data.

For an additional fee, the database will include the suppliers "Sales Agent" Software called DataFind. DataFind will provide an additional analysis of customer information with the aim of predicting future sales to individual customers. The promotional material on DataFind includes the following graph, showing the cost and value of information.

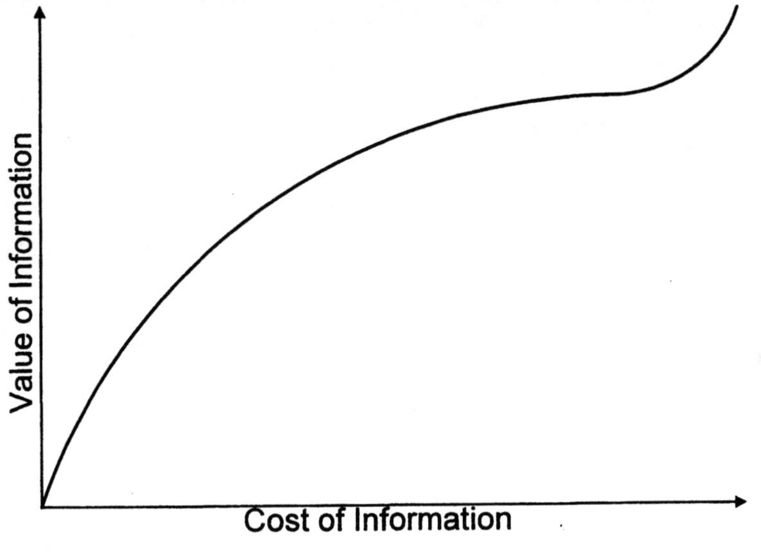

As a junior management accountant in TT you have been asked to perform the tasks outlined below.

Required:

(a) Evaluate the relationship between the cost and value of information, with specific reference to the graph above showing the benefit of the DataFind software.

(9 marks)

(b) Discuss the costs and benefits that would help to determine whether the purchase of the sales software should proceed.

NOTE: You are not required to state any financial information for inclusion in the CBA.

(16 marks)

(Total = 25 marks)

Question Four

The VG organisation has 24 offices in various locations within one country; its main activity is selling replacement windows and doors. Each office maintains its own information systems but sends financial summaries to Head Office on a daily basis. Information provided by Head Office includes financial targets and summaries as well as updates on products for onward transmission to sales representatives.

Each VG office employs up to 50 sales representatives. The method of selling is for the representative to visit a potential customer and produce a detailed specification for windows and doors for their property. Details for the specification are obtained either from paper-based reference material maintained by each representative, or by telephoning technical design specialists at Head Office prior to the specification being completed. Completed specifications for each customer order processed are sent back to Head Office in the post. All companies in the industry use a similar approach.

Sales representatives work from home. They visit their office only for occasional training courses and to obtain updates on their reference material for windows and doors.

Delays in producing the specification document can occur due to:

- The paper records maintained by the sales representatives being out of date.
- Poor communication and misunderstanding between the sales representatives and the Head Office design specialists.

While 98% of specifications are produced on time, the remaining 2% are delayed resulting in poor customer relations and publicity. Removing the delays would therefore be appropriate.

The IT department in the VG organisation has suggested that various IT systems could be used to assist communication and provide access to databases on windows and doors. However, no firm proposals have yet been made.

Required:

(a) Discuss the barriers in the VG organisation to achieving effective communication and to using IT in order to provide access to databases in the VG organisation.

(10 marks)

(b)

(i) Discuss how IS / IT can be used to obtain competitive advantage in the VG organisation.

(10 marks)

(ii) Explain the factors the Board needs to consider in order to determine whether or not to upgrade the system.

(5 marks)

(Total for requirement (b) = 15 marks)

(Total = 25 marks)

Question Five

You have joined a rapidly expanding company as a trainee management accountant. Your job is to report to the senior management accountant on the production activities of the company on a weekly basis. However, this is a new job and you are the first person appointed to it. As a result there are no existing information systems available to you.

Required:

(a) Discuss how you will determine the information requirements for your new job. Use examples from your own employment or appropriate industry examples to support your answer.

(12 marks)

(b) The senior management accountant has indicated that the company has no effective IS strategy. Discuss the problems of setting an IS strategy in a rapidly expanding company.

(13 marks)

(Total = 25 marks)

End of paper

The Examiner for FLIS offers to future candidates and to lecturers using this booklet for study purposes, the following background and guidance on the questions included in this examination paper.

Section A – compulsory

Question One part (a) tests candidates' ability to identify weaknesses of information systems which is essential so that recommendations can be made later to overcome those weaknesses. This question uses the value chain to help the candidate provide an appropriate structure to their answer and then, in practice, assist other people in reading and understanding the report. Part (b) assumes candidates will have knowledge of the different support systems available to manage information and this part tests their ability to demonstrate that knowledge of a specific system, with the ability to explain the qualities of information expected from that system. Part (c): Candidates will be aware of the different systems development available, including internal and external sourcing. This part allows candidates to evaluate whether one particular development methodology is appropriate for a specific situation. Part (d): Candidates will be aware that to be used effectively, an IT system must be accepted by the people who will use it. This part allows candidates to discuss factors that will affect the decision by staff to use a specific system.

Section B – two questions from four

Question Two part (a): Candidates will be familiar with "bricks and mortar" companies establishing Internet divisions. This part allows candidates to consider whether the reverse situation could occur and therefore advise managers on the appropriate course of action to take. Part (b): Candidates will realise that part of the benefit of IT is being able to justify the implementation in terms of quantifiable results. This part allows candidates to demonstrate this knowledge in terms of setting CSF's and the associated PI's to help determine the success of the diversification into retail bookshops.

Question Three part (a): One of the impacts of IT systems is the ability to provide information quicker, but at a price. Companies, therefore, need to justify expenditure to obtain additional information. This part allows candidates to justify the expenditure using non-financial methods. Part (b): Cost Benefit Analysis is one of the main tools to justify an investment in information systems. In this scenario, as in many situations involving information systems, the candidate needs to identify the intangible benefits to try and justify the investment in information systems.

Question Four part (a): Candidates will be familiar with the problems of co-ordination in a decentralised organisation. This part uses a specific example of staff not being able to communicate effectively where IT is currently not used to any great extent. Barriers to co-ordination therefore relate partly to the organisation structure but also to the social issues of lack of experience and use of IT in the specific situation. Part (b): Candidates will be familiar with the need to use IS/IT to obtain competitive advantage in different industries. This part allows candidates to demonstrate how IS/IT could be used in situations where currently very little use is made of IT. However, there may be no easy solution to using IT in the scenario and candidates should also not be afraid of pointing this out in their answers.

Question Five part (a): Candidates should be familiar with their information requirements, no matter what type of employment they are in. This question allows candidates to show how information requirements for their job can be determined, allowing practical experience to be used in their answers. Part (b): Candidates will be familiar with the need for an IS strategy from the work of Earl. This part requires more than simply re-iterating the theory as examples must be provided from a rapidly expanding company.

CIMA

The Examiner's Answers for Management Accounting – Information Strategy

SECTION A

Answer to Question One

Requirement (a)

Characteristics of information of the EIS include:

Accurate
Information should be accurate to an appropriate level of detail. An EIS would normally be expected to show summarised information, perhaps to the nearest £10,000 or sometimes millions of pounds. Given that the output from the EIS appears to be contract prices to the nearest pound, rather than a summary, the EIS is not providing information to the appropriate level of detail.

Complete
Completeness implies that all the information required is actually being given to the Board. However, completeness in terms of an EIS may not be possible simply because information may not be available due to the nature of Board decision making. In JA's EIS, the information may be complete in terms of a listing of contracts, there is simply not enough detail to make this decision. However, it is probably not complete in terms of identifying those contracts that need attention.

Concise
Conciseness implies that the information can be easily assimilated or understood by the recipient. In JA this may not be the case because it is not clear what the information means e.g. the letters for stage of production. Conciseness has been taken too far in this instance and additional detail is required.

User-friendly
User-friendly implies that information can be understood by the recipient, or it is in a format that they would expect. In terms of the JA EIS, this is not the case. Board reports are normally formatted with graphs to show trends, rather than lists of items or numbers. Re-formatting the report would therefore be recommended.

Relevant
Information should be relevant to the job function of the recipient. The output from the JA EIS appears to be a relatively low level report produced for junior or middle management in order to control production rather than high level summary of production for senior management. The output from the EIS is therefore no longer relevant to the Board.

Authoritative
Information should have authority, that is, it should be trustworthy; this normally means that information has been derived from an appropriate source. For an EIS, this will normally mean information will be obtained from internal and external sources, and also checked prior to being given to the Board to ensure it is correct. Information in the EIS has been derived from internal sources and presumably checked, so it does meet this criterion.

Timely
Information should be provided at an appropriate time so that decisions can be made. Information from an EIS is not normally time constrained due to the longer term nature of the decision making. There is no indication on the example output of the timescale of the report or the production date/time; it is therefore difficult to comment on the timeliness of the information.

Easy to use
Finally, information should overall be easy to use. Given the comments made above, it is clear that the EIS no longer meets this criterion.

Requirement (b)

Weaknesses of current systems

Most of the weaknesses of the current systems appear to relate to the operations section of the value chain.

Inbound logistics – Loss of economies of scale in purchasing
Within the CPD, it appears that quotes are obtained for each individual order. While this may be efficient regarding obtaining the quote, the JA company will lose any possibility of gaining economies of scale from bulk purchases, unless some agreement is reached with suppliers at the beginning of the year for bulk discount on purchases to be made.

Operations – CRM and stock system
The CRM and stock systems do not appear to be linked. The CRM obtains information about individual orders but stock availability is only checked from the Central Purchasing Department after order details have been transferred from the CRM. Given that sales representatives apparently use the CRM as a basis for making quotes on each vat, this system has weaknesses such as:

- The quote for the vat may be incorrect. Representatives are relying on their knowledge of materials from previous quotes rather than actual prices being maintained in the CPD. An incorrect quote may result in a loss being made on production, or the order for a vat not being obtained because the price quoted is too high.
- Unrealistic lead times for delivery of vats may be provided. The sales representatives do not have access to actual materials availability or production capacity in the JA company. As a result, unrealistic estimates of delivery dates may be provided, unless the sales representatives liaise carefully with the production department.

Operations – Transfer of information CRM to CPD
Information on the production requirements for each vat is transferred from the CRM to the CPD by email. Use of e-mail in this situation may be inappropriate because there is no automatic tracking of order details between the two systems. For example:

- E-mails do not automatically have any form of numeric sequence, making it difficult if not impossible to monitor completeness of transfer of individual orders from the CRM to the CPD.
- E-mail delivery may not be monitored, resulting in entire orders being lost. The use of a third party ISP is potentially risky at this stage simply because there are more steps to transfer each e-mail increasing the risk of loss.
- It is not clear what action needs to be taken if it is found that a particular vat cannot be manufactured. Presumably the sales representatives should be informed of this problem. However, it is not clear how information is transferred back from the CPD to the CRM.

Operations – Lack of job scheduling
The parts for each vat are sent to production as and when they become available. While CAD/CAM is being used to assist in the manufacture of each vat, there does not appear to be any job or production scheduling. This may result in the following problems:

- Production of individual vats being delayed because too many orders are sent to production at once. Delivery estimates provided by sales representatives for each vat may also therefore be incorrect, unless the representatives check order process with the production department. Production cost may also be increased if overtime is incurred.
- Periods when productive capacity is not being used, resulting in the CAD/CAM system standing idle.

Operations – Materials availability from shops
After an order is received in the CPD, availability of materials from shops is checked. It is not clear at this stage whether materials are actually allocated to the production of individual vats, or whether simply shops are checked for those materials. If the latter system is in place then when the manufacture of a specific vat is started, it is possible that the materials from shops are no longer available; they may have been allocated to a different vat. This weakness will have the effect of further delaying production while the shop materials are obtained.

Marketing and sales - Invoicing of vats
The accounts department is made aware of the need to invoice for a specific vat by the receipt of an email from the CPD. On the assumption that this email is routed via an external ISP, then the system suffers from the same weaknesses as the link from the CRM to the CPD. In this situation, additional problems that may occur include:

- Goods being despatched without being invoiced, as delivery information is not confirmed as being received in accounts. This will understate sales for the JA Company and possible non-receipt of cash representing the order value.
- The statutory accounts and any internal information regarding the sales and profitability of the company will be incorrect. However, it appears that the CRM is used to supply details of sales and purchases for each vat. Failure to record a vat sale in accounts would therefore result in a discrepancy between the CRM and accounts. Given there is no link between these two systems, then the error will not be identified.

Requirement (c)

Outsourcing the development of the new EIS may be appropriate for the JA Company for the following reasons:

Core business
Maintaining the EIS is not directly related to the core business of the JA Company. The company's main business is producing vats. Attempting to produce the EIS in-house may divert resources and attention away from the core business causing this to fail.

Budget
A budget has been agreed for the new EIS, although it is not clear exactly what is included in this budget. In-house may be less inclined to attempt to meet the budget, because their own salaries and to some extent career development may not be linked to this. Budget overruns may therefore occur. An outsourcing company, however, will need to meet an agreed budget. Outsourcing provides more certainty that the budget will be met.

Skills available
It appears that there is insufficient in-house skill to produce the new EIS. Commencement of any project will therefore be delayed by hiring new staff. Lack of skill at this stage also overcomes one of the normal problems with outsourcing, namely that external staff will not have full knowledge of company systems. As there already is lack of knowledge, there is no additional problem in hiring a third party.

Error correction
Even if the JA Company manages to recruit the necessary staff, there is no guarantee that they will continue to work for the company after the new EIS has been written. IT staff may see this as close of a project, and move on to the next challenge. If this happens, then JA will be left without appropriate IT support for the EIS. Outsourcing the project should mean that the outsourcer will be able to provide ongoing support because knowledge of the EIS will remain in that company, even if development staff do leave.

Outsourcing may not be appropriate for the following reasons:

Lack of specification
The lack of specification tends to indicate that the directors are not exactly clear what they would like from the EIS. It may therefore be more appropriate to use in-house staff to develop the EIS because they will be able to determine the directors' requirements more precisely, and use tacit knowledge of the company to produce a more appropriate EIS. External staff will not have this knowledge and may therefore make errors in the specification. At the very least, a detailed review of the specification will be required in-house to ensure that it is accurate.

Lack of user acceptance
One of the keys to obtaining acceptance of any new system is to involve staff in system design. Given that the MDD Company has already suggested an off-the-shelf system, then it is unlikely that full consultation with JA staff has been undertaken, and so staff may reject the system.

Lack of experience
It is not clear what experience MDD has either with designing EIS or with the particular industry that JA Company operates in. Lack of experience may result in production of inappropriate software. If outsourcing is to be undertaken, then at least two other quotes from other vendors are required to ensure that skill sets and experience can be fully compared.

Requirement (d)

Staff are likely to accept changes to the systems for the following reasons:

Current systems
It is recognised that the current systems do not provide the necessary information at any management level. Staff are likely to accept the change, simply because it is expected and seen to be necessary. Staff are therefore more likely to be tolerant of any disruption in systems change than would normally be the case.

New systems may not be accepted for the following reasons:

EIS v TPS
Staff using the TPS may not want to wait until the EIS has been amended to have the different TPS's updated. While it is clear that the EIS has some major weaknesses, initial focus on this system implies, rightly or wrongly, that it is more important that the TPS. Directors may be advised to amend the TPS first to avoid any "badwill" with the update of the EIS.

Issues with centralised system
It appears that the current system causes significant delays partly from the system structure and partly from the age of the hardware. Purchase of an off-the-shelf system would appear to focus on the software requirements for the system change and not necessarily on the hardware or system structure. Care must be taken to ensure that the hardware is also upgraded as necessary. New software is likely to require more processing power than old so there is a significant danger that the new system will run even slower.

Staff expectations
Staff expects both the new TPS and the EIS to alleviate the current problems. Care must be taken to ensure that the new systems do meet those expectations. It may be better to under-sell the systems rather than suggest all problems will be fixed as this will help acceptability later.

Lack of user involvement
The decision to accept off-the-shelf packages may appear to be cost effective and provide a quick implementation. However, this decision may also create resentment amongst users as they will not be involved in the system design. Lack of input may also mean lack of system acceptance when it is finally implemented. Rather than jump straight to the answer of an off-the-shelf system, views of staff should be obtained and the system checked to ensure it meets their expectations. Staff will therefore feel part of the overall change and more likely to accept any new system.

Amend work practices to suit the system
Amending work practices without initial user involvement is also likely to be unacceptable to staff. This will be a specific problem where new practices are seen to be less efficient, or provide illogical work methods. Again, user involvement is needed at the system design stage to ensure that the human aspects of process are included in the system design.

SECTION B

Answer to Question Two

Requirement (a)

Link to business strategy of company

Initially, the Board must consider whether the purchase of bookshops actually fits with the overall strategy of the company. While NLE has been successful on the Internet, this does not necessary mean it will be successful in a "bricks and mortar" situation. Care must be taken to ensure that purchase of the shops does not detract from the successful Internet operations, or worse, cause the company to fail.

Information on the business and information strategies will be available from previous Board meetings. Some form of cash and profit forecast would be useful to determine the expected result from the new venture.

Amendment of current Internet site – allow ordering from shops and collect from shop
NLE's information systems will need amending to ensure that orders can be received from the shops, and that customers can place orders on the Internet for later collection at the shop. While this may appear to be a simple change, a programme change specification must be produced identifying the changes required and then the timescales and cost of change determined.

The information required is therefore the program specification itself along with a list of the expected costs for the new hardware. The latter will include provision of a WAN and any upgrade costs to existing hardware at the bookshops to ensure that they can be connected to the online systems.

Incompatible systems – shops and Internet
Given that NLE has had no contact with the bookshops, it is extremely likely that the computer systems will be different both in terms of hardware and software. Lack of compatibility may mean that either new hardware will have to be purchased in the shops, or that NLE's existing software will have to be loaded onto the "old" hardware. Again, an option must be chosen and the costs determined.

Information will be obtained from an audit of the current hardware. This will be compared to the specification for the new system to determine whether existing hardware is sufficient for the new system. Where this is not the case then a list of required new hardware with indicative cost will be required.

Effect on e-business
The effect on the e-business must be considered. Given that the e-business is profitable, appropriate management time must be devoted to this division to ensure profitability continues. The effect on the NLE brand on opening shops must also be checked; while the brand name is known now, market research may be needed to ensure that the brand will not suffer from maintaining bookshops. Similarly, the Board must ensure that the high standard of service expected from NLE from using the website can be maintained in the shops.

Information on this area will be difficult to obtain. As noted above, market research may be used to determine the effect on the brand name of NLE. However, there appear to be few examples of internet business moving into bricks and mortar making the proposed change riskier than expected.

Requirement (b)

The overall mission of NLE is *to be the most reliable and cost efficient supplier of books and CDs on the Internet.* It is therefore appropriate to link the CSFs and PIs to this mission statement, changing the statement slightly to reflect the different purchasing medium.

Reliable supplier
CSF – Shop customers satisfied with product fulfilment.

PI – 95% of shop purchases available either on day of sale or next day in-shop.

Comment
To be reliable, NLE needs to ensure that the same product range from the Internet is also available to shop customers. Satisfied customers will provide repeat business; however, lack of order fulfilment will damage the NLE brand name.

Cost efficient supplier
CSF – Bookshops to make a positive contribution to the NLE organisation.

PI – Bookshops to earn a 20% net profit after one year.

Comment
Technically, this CSF should be external and compare the results from the NLE shops to other organisations. However, comparative information may not be available, limiting the effectiveness of the CSF. Providing some internal performance measurement of net profit will at least ensure that the bookshops are making a net contribution to the NLE organisation. The effect of customers transferring from Internet to shops may also have to be considered regarding the overall profitability of the company. Note that PI must be quantifiable.

Answer to Question Three

Requirement (a)

The general relationship between cost and value of information, as shown on the graph, is that as the value of information increases, so the cost of providing that information also increases.

However, this relationship is not always linear. Any initial expenditure on information systems will have a relatively good payback, in that information will be provided for the first time, so the value of that information will be relatively large. Then, as more money is invested in information systems, so the value of information produced becomes less and less. This is explained by the information systems already producing the information needed by decision makers; any additional information is useful, but does not significantly affect their decisions.

Eventually, there is a time when too much information is being produced and the extra investment in information provides no additional value. This occurs on the graph where the line becomes parallel to the x-axis.

The relationship in this graph is unusual because it implies that the value of information starts to increase again. The explanation for this relationship is likely to be the DataFind module in the sales software. DataFind appears to be some sort of intelligent agent software. This software searches a database (or a number of related databases) to try and find "hidden" relationships within that data. For example, there may be a link between a customer's postcode and the CD's that they purchase. With this information, TT could send out specific mailshots (perhaps in addition to emails) to the customer with information on new CDs that they might be interested in; hopefully the result of this action will be increased purchases and therefore increased contribution for TT.

However, there is a critical mass of data that will be required before these relationships become apparent. This implies that a lot of data will have to be stored in the database before the use of intelligent agents is effective. So, having paid for the basic sales software, and populated the database, some additional expenditure on DataFind will result in increased value of information; hence the curve moves up again towards the end of the graph.

Requirement (b)

Cost and benefits of the new sales system

Costs
Costs of the new system will include:

System changeover Costs in this category will include converting the sales ledger balances onto the new system and then integrating the sales software with the stock system.

New system hardware Given that the original sales system was implemented four years ago, it is likely that new or upgraded hardware will be required to run the new system. At the least, additional memory will be needed to run the enhancements to the system.

The new software will have to be purchased, *including* the DataFind module, if this is required.

Staff training may be required where the functionality of the systems are significantly different. Some basic training is advisable anyway to ensure that sales staff understand the system and are motivated to use it.

DataFind software, if purchased.

Benefits
Cost savings. Savings of not operating the old sales systems.
Some of these savings will be tangible such as the reduction in staff costs, possibly due to direct interface between the stock and the sales systems.

Benefits relate to the operation of the new sales system. Many benefits will be intangible and therefore difficult to quantify. Benefits will include:

- Access to the customer information will now be quicker and easier. This implies that sales staff will be more productive in answering customer queries resulting in better customer service. There may also be further staff savings if fewer customer service staff are required.
- Improved customer service may result in increased sales revenue, providing additional contribution to the organisation. Customers are more likely to make repeat purchases when they have received good customer service.
- Improved staff morale as they are better able to deal with customer queries. Improved morale will also have a beneficial effect on customer service. Customers will recognise that staff are motivated and helpful and so return to make repeat purchases.
- Improved decision making resulting from improved knowledge of customer purchasing habits. The ability to track total sales of individual CD's will help to produce a profile of the history of sales of each CD. Stock management will be improved because the stock of CD's can be matched to the expected sales profile. Two benefits will arise from this action. First, CD's are likely to be in stock when ordered, and so despatch is quicker. Secondly, customer service will improved as customers will receive their CD's quicker.
- Ability to direct marketing opportunities direct to the individual customer. Using past purchasing history, DataFind will be able to forecast which CD's each customer will be interested in purchasing. Information about these CD's can be provided next time the customer logs onto the website, via direct e-mail to that customer or possibly by mailshot.

Answer to Question Four

Requirement (a)

Barriers to effective communication
The current system involves using the telephone as the main communication channel. This may be inappropriate for the following reasons:

Technical information
The telephone may not effective for communicating detailed technical information. It will be easy to make mistakes either in explaining the information or in recording. Some form of channel allowing transfer of text would to be more appropriate as the actual technical specifications could be referred to.

Availability of staff
Use of the telephone assumes a technical design specialist will be available to answer telephone calls and respond to queries. This may not be the case as the specialist may be at break or there are simply too many telephone calls. Stopping work to take a telephone call may also interrupt the work of the specialist unnecessarily. Provision of a system to allow messages to be accessed and read at the convenience of the specialist, such as e-mail, would ensure that the messages were received and that the specialist could act on them when convenient for the specialist.

Decentralised system
Use of a decentralised system will mean duplicated information being stored in different databases, for example, customers and stock information. This will make comparison of data very difficult.

Data formats
The use of decentralised systems may also result in databases having different formats. Provision of a standard format will again assist comparison and amalgamation of information.

Delay in distribution
The system almost certainly incorporates delays in distributing information from centre to representatives. Data is presumably sent via each location then onto the representatives. The result of this is that data on windows and doors could be out of date due to transmission delays.

Philosophy of sales representatives.
Sales representatives are not used to using computers. They may therefore not accept a new system using computers or use it inappropriately limiting the effectiveness of their job.

Location
Representatives work in many different locations. The company therefore cannot determine exactly what communication systems will be available, especially whether telephone lines for use of e-mail could be used. This will limit the effectiveness of any revised system by incorporating delays as well as uncertainty of use.

Update of databases
Representatives are not office based, meaning that they will have to update product databases from remote locations. Some procedure will be needed and discipline required to try and ensure that databases on each laptop are updated regularly.

IT appropriate?
No work study done showing whether or not IT is actually appropriate, there are only indications from the IT department that this may be a suitable system. Additional time needs to be spent on a feasibility study to check that the system is actually appropriate.

Requirement (b)

(i) Use of IT is difficult because of the problems noted in part *(a)*, particularly issues such as lack of access to networks inherent in remote working. However, IS/IT may provide some competitive advantage at various levels within the company, as outlined below:

Form completion
Representatives will have to complete standard documentation as a basis for each customer order. This documentation can be computerised, based on standard forms. While this is unlikely to provide any specific competitive advantage as most companies computerise basic input documents, failure to use computer-generated forms may provide an adverse view of the company, limiting sales opportunities.

Numeric control of orders
Using computer generated forms may have the added advantage of allowing automatic numbering of those forms. This will assist in the tracking of orders, as well as providing computer generated exception reports on missing orders or orders which are behind schedule.

Display of products
Access can be provided to the database of specifications on the representatives' laptop at customer premises. As well as being up-to-date, the computer can store images of different windows and doors and possibly show short videos of installation techniques or examples of properties with the windows and doors fitted. However, there will be a need for a method of updating files on laptop although this could be provided by remote access each evening.

Communication
E-mail could be used for communication to a technical design specialist although this is unlikely to provide competitive advantage regarding response times due to problems of connectivity. However, e-mail would provide documentation of queries, and copies could be forwarded to the customers e-mail account to show progress of those queries.

Expert system
There is the possibility of using Expert System on laptop to advise on design issues. In effect, the representative could feed in details of the window or door required, such as size and location in the house, and the Expert System provides examples of the type of door or window required. While this may appear to be useful, it may detract from the human aspect of selling doors and windows and would probably be expensive to produce.

Text messages
An alternative to e-mail would be the use of text messaging to design specialists. While this removes the problem of connectability, text messages take longer to write and may not be suitable for more complicated technical queries.

Output of specifications
Use of a portable colour printer would enable sales representatives to leave copies of any forms and other documents produced showing the window/door types to be used with the customer. Alternatively, the customer could be provided with a link to the company's website where those forms could be found.

(ii) In deciding whether or not to amend the IT systems, the Board of VG will need to work through the following process:

- Determine the business needs of the organisation.
- Check whether IT can be used to support this objective. In this situation, selling windows and doors is the main objective of VG; any use of IT must support this objective.
- Obtain a cost benefit analysis of the different IT options available to the company.

Many of the ideas mentioned above may appear to support the business, but they also suffer from some shortcomings and in some situations such as the use of Expert Systems are likely to be expensive. There is a need therefore to check how much benefit will actually be derived.

If any systems do provide benefit, then the Board of VG must decide whether to implement the IT system and allocate an appropriate budget. Appropriate resources in terms of people and time must also be made available.

The system should be developed involving the sales representatives. As they have not used computers in their work before, it is essential to ensure that the representatives are "on board" to avoid system failure from lack of use.

Finally, implementation could be carried out on a pilot basis to ensure that a sample of representatives is satisfied with the system, prior to rollout to the whole company.

Answer to Question Five

Requirement (a)

Determining new job information requirements

Job specification
Initially, I would need to determine exactly what my job entails. This will mean obtaining my job specification and checking exactly what things must be done (that is determine my own Critical Success Factors) to meet that specification. For example, there may be specific reports to produce or people to report to. My own CSF would then relate to providing appropriate reporting to these people.

Discussions with senior management accountant
Having identified who I am reporting to, it would be useful to discuss with the senior management accountant and any other people exactly what reports are required. Specific report formats and content along with timing of reports can then be determined. This will tell me exactly what outputs I have to produce.

Company CSF
It may also be useful to check with company objectives to see what the CSF's and PI's are to ensure these are being monitored by appropriate people including the senior management accountant. While this is not meant to be second-guessing the work of the senior management accountant, a fresh pair of eyes is sometimes useful in ensuring that objectives are being met.

Information needed
Having determined what reports need to be produced, and in what format, a list of the information required to produce those reports can be determined. This information may well come from internal and external sources. For example, a report on sales is likely to show sales against budget in the company with additional information on market share from analysis of competitors or obtaining industry data.

Obtain information
Finally, I will need to find out where the information I need to produce the reports can be obtained. The company will already have some information systems which will hopefully provide the necessary information. For example, details of sales (to assist forecast sales and therefore production activities) will be obtained from the sales system, or sales ledger control in the nominal ledger. However, other sources may be missing, such as external information on competitors. If this is the case, then arrangements will have to be made to obtain the information. Where this involves additional expense, such as Internet access, then the senior accountant will need to approve the expenditure.

Check for completeness
A further check for completeness of information can be carried out after the first reports are produced. Discussions with the senior accountant will highlight any omissions and these can hopefully be remedied for subsequent reports.

Requirement (b)

The problems of setting an IS strategy in a rapidly expanding company will include:

Budget
The difficulty here is how to keep IT expenditure in check when budgets are set annually and IT requirements may change monthly. There may need to be a method of flexing or amending budget regularly to allow for new systems or purchase of equipment for new staff that was not foreseen when the initial budget is set. The overall requirement is that business development is not hindered simply because staff cannot have the necessary tools to carry out their jobs effectively.

Systems change
The systems of the company may change regularly (note new trainee accountant does not have an IT system) as the requirements of uses change, departments expand and so on. This means that new Information Systems will be needed on a regular basis. The challenge will be ensuring that these systems remain compatible and can share appropriate information.

IT as an enabling technology
Various opportunities for use of IT may be noted in different sections of the company. This may encourage individual development of the systems to suit the needs of one section of the company or provide competitive advantage for one division. While this may provide a suitable system, other sections of the organisation may not be aware of this and therefore provide different systems or level of service. Overall service will be compromised where customers see different levels of service being provided.

Management information
IS strategy aims to provide management with the information they need when it is needed. This may be difficult where systems are changing, particularly as the EIS may not be sufficiently well integrated into new or amended systems to provide management with the information that they require.

Customers
Customers will require information on products ordered, stage of production, delivery dates, after sales service and so on. The IS strategy must therefore provide an appropriate Customer Relationship Management system to track details of customer orders, requirements and so on. If systems are changing or being amended, then there is a danger that information will be lost resulting in poor customer relations. Care will be needed to maintain the integrity of information at all times.

IT systems
Rapid growth may mean that systems suddenly become unusable due to excessive file sizes or volume of processing. The IS strategy must try and recognise these problems in advance by monitoring closely the usage of IT in the organisation. Where system failure is likely, additional resource will have to be allocated to avoid system breakdown.

CIMA

November 2004 Examinations

Final Level

Management Accounting – Case Study

(FLCS – Paper 15)

The answers published here have been written by the Case Writer and should provide a helpful guide for both lecturers and students.

Published separately on the CIMA website (www.cimaglobal.com/students) from the end of March 2005 is a Post Examination Guide for this paper, which provides much valuable and complementary material including indicative mark information.

CIMA

Final Level Management Accounting – Case Study

15 FLCS

INSTRUCTIONS FOR POTENTIAL CANDIDATES

This booklet contains the ***pre-seen case material*** for the November 2004 examination. It will provide you with context information that will help you to prepare yourself for the examination on 25 November.
You may not take this copy of the pre-seen material into the examination hall. A fresh copy will be provided in the examination hall.
The Assessment Matrix is available separately on the website, as is guidance on how to prepare for the examination. The matrix will also be provided in the examination hall.
Unseen material will be provided for the examination: this will comprise further context information and the examination question.
The examination will last for three hours.
You will be required to answer one question, which may contain more than one element.

Contents: *Page*

Mayah Group of Hospitals

1. Introduction and context for change

The Mayah Group of Hospitals (MGH) is a public sector organisation operating over three sites in the north of Zamorna, a fictitious country in Western Europe. This part of the country is affluent and the population has a better than average state of general health. There are, however, pockets of deprivation where there is a higher than average incidence of some types of disease and "life style" ailments such as obesity and smoking-related illnesses. The demographic profile of the region covered by MGH is shown in *Appendix A*. MGH is not the only public sector hospital in the region, but it is by far the largest and offers the widest range of services.

In Zamorna, health services are provided by a combination of public and private sector organisations. The public sector providers, such as MGH, are financed by a mixture of national and local taxation and most treatments are free to the patient at the point of delivery. However, the current government has encouraged greater private sector participation in a variety of ways, for example in providing finance for new buildings and, recently, by using (and paying for) private sector facilities to supplement those provided by the public sector. More contentiously, it is considering allowing expenditure on private healthcare and health insurance premiums paid by individuals to be partially tax deductible. A sizeable minority of the population is able to afford private healthcare or health insurance.

The Zamorna government has determined a range of objectives and targets that public sector providers must achieve. The objectives deal broadly with the efficiency and effectiveness of healthcare in the context of improving health and obtaining value for money. On many performance measures, both clinical and managerial, MGH has demonstrated a worse performance than the majority of hospitals of similar size in areas of similar demographic profile. Not only is it worse than other comparable organisations, but also in many areas of service its performance is declining.

The MGH Board had for some time recognised that its poor performance was largely for the following reasons:

- *(i)* the increasing cost of providing services from three separate sites;
- *(ii)* the changing health needs of the local population;
- *(iii)* poor human resource relations with all categories of staff, partly because of poor communications and partly because of poor working conditions.

There is also a shortage of good, qualified staff but this problem is common throughout the country.

The need to achieve more cost-effective provision and improved quality of clinical services has been a key feature of Board discussions for some time. However, the real impetus for change was the government's demand for a thorough strategic review of its operations. This was concluded six months ago and major redevelopment and reorganisation has become inevitable.

2. Organisation and management structure and corporate objectives

2.1 Organisation structure

There are three hospitals in the group under the same management. The main areas of business of these three hospitals are explained below. The group as a whole employs around 5,500 staff (full-time equivalents), 75% of whom are in clinical professions.

The district hospital (DH)

This is the largest hospital in the group. It provides a wide range of medical and surgical procedures from minor operations to treatment of major illnesses and injuries. Certain specialised procedures, such as organ transplants, are referred to the main regional infirmary or a specialist hospital in another part of the country.

DH treats around 52,000 in-patients a year. It also has an out-patient facility treating around 160,000 patients a year and an accident and emergency department treating 85,000 casualties a year.

The average length of stay of in-patients in this hospital is 3 to 4 days, but there is a very large variation. The majority of treatment episodes are one- or two-day stays but some patients with serious illnesses or injuries may be there for six months or more.

The mental hospital (MH)

This hospital caters for patients with mental illnesses and psychological problems and disorders. It also provides residential rehabilitation and detoxification facilities for patients suffering from substance abuse. It has capacity for 150 in-patients and also provides day clinics to assist patients maintain their state of health once they have been discharged from residential treatment programmes. Many of its patients are from neighbouring districts as it is the only hospital in the region providing this type of facility.

It suffers from a disadvantage of being located some distance from the Mayah city centre and transport services and other amenities are poor. This means many people in need of the clinic's services are frequently unable or unwilling to travel to the clinic.

The maternity and child welfare clinic (MCWC)

This clinic provides maternity and child welfare services. In an average year, the clinic will have 2,500 deliveries and treat 4,500 children for various illnesses and diseases. The number of deliveries is likely to decrease over the next few years due to the changing demographics of the region and the increase in popularity of home births and use of private sector clinics.

Typically, new mothers leave hospital within two days of the birth of their child unless there is a complication. Most children are treated as out-patients. If their condition is serious or requires major surgery, they are referred to the children's ward of the district hospital.

2.2 History of current organisation

The current configuration of hospitals has come about by accident rather than by managerial design. Until 10 years ago, the two hospitals and the clinic were three separate organisations with their own management board and funding streams. The government of the day was keen to reduce the costs of managing and administering health services and had forced the three boards to review their management structures and operations.

In 1995, in response to these government pressures, a consultation paper was issued that suggested merging the maternity and child welfare services with a similar clinic in a neighbouring district. The neighbouring clinic would provide maternity services and Mayah clinic child welfare. There was also a proposal to re-site the mental health services hospital to a low-usage building within the district hospital complex. This would provide a much more accessible location and allow considerable cost savings.

The financial and organisational logic was compelling but the public outcry to both sets of proposals resulted in them being abandoned. A compromise solution was to merge the three organisations' management under the current organisational structure. This allowed some cost savings but did nothing to improve the service levels. There are now serious tensions within the organisation, mainly between clinical and administrative staff, that have led to a high staff turnover in recent years and a difficulty in recruitment.

A further problem is the age and condition of the district hospital's buildings. The main building was built over 80 years ago and does not lend itself to the major renovations necessary to provide the facilities required by modern hospitals. The other peripheral buildings are newer but they are spread out around the city and most are in need of refurbishment.

2.3 *Management structure*

The MGH Board currently has nine members – four executive and five non-executive Directors. There is a vacancy for a sixth non-executive Director that has been unfilled for over twelve months. Brief details of the Board are as follows:

Executive Directors:

Chief Executive: John Asta has worked in the hospital sector since leaving university with a degree in biotechnology. He started his career as a clinician and moved into management eight years ago. He has been Chief Executive of MGH since 2001.

Director of Finance and Performance Measurement: Olivia Owulu is a qualified management accountant and holds an MBA from an American business school. She worked in the private sector until five years ago when she was headhunted for this position.

Director of Human Resources: Dolores Rossiter is a recent recruit to MGH. She is an American citizen who moved to Zamorna last year with her husband who is a consultant anaesthetist, also now working for MGH.

Director of Planning: Georges Papadopoulous is the longest serving member of the Board. He was a senior manager at the maternity hospital before it merged with Mayah. The responsibilities for planning were until that time undertaken by the Director of Finance. The decision to split the role and award Georges a director's post led to the resignation of the then Director of Finance and the appointment of Olivia Owulu.

Non-Executive Directors (all part-time appointments):

Non-Executive Chairman: Professor Frances Cluna is a full time academic at the local university. Her area of expertise is pharmacy and pharmacology. She is also politically astute and understands the political imperatives of managing any public sector organisation. She has been Chairman for three years.

She has known John Asta since university and it was as a result of his invitation that she applied for and was appointed to the position of Chairman.

Non-Executive Directors

Brigitte Binardi is a retired social worker who has been a non-executive director on a variety of health sector boards. She is also actively involved in voluntary work in health-related charities. She is an advocate of MGH maintaining a full service provision, and wholly opposed to private sector involvement in the health service. This frequently brings her into conflict with colleagues who generally take a more pragmatic view and accept change is inevitable.

Carlos Cluntz is a local businessman who runs his own successful computer company that specialises in systems and software design. He is a relative newcomer to the role of non-executive having joined the Board only six months ago. He is frustrated by the administrative complexities and bureaucracies inherent in hospital management.

Dr Indira Mehra is an industrial chemist who works full time for a large pharmaceutical company. She has been a non-executive director at MGH for three years and Vice Chair for the past twelve months, although she has been ill for much of the past six months.

John Vance is a freelance stress management consultant. His business involves delivering one-day seminars to employees of client companies and also individual stress counselling, contracted either by organisations for their staff or by individuals.

2.4 *Corporate aims*

The MGH Annual Report states that the Group has four main aims within its overall mission, which is *"To serve the people of the region by improving standards of health and providing high quality services"*. The four main aims are:

- to deliver high quality healthcare to the residents of the region in which MGH operates;
- to provide value for money in terms of output per € spent;
- to improve the health of the local population by the use of pro-active measures;
- to recognise the needs of all the organisation's stakeholders and treat them with equal respect.

With the possible exception of value for money, these objectives are not quantified and are difficult to measure. When Carlos Cluntz joined the Board of MGH he felt little more than lip service was paid to these objectives and he attempted to persuade his fellow Directors that it was necessary to translate them into tangible goals and actions. To help achieve this, he argued for the introduction of a balanced scorecard approach. He has not had much success; the pressure of dealing with frequent "urgent" management issues meant that merely important issues were usually forgotten or ignored.

3. Future service needs and proposals for change

The strategic review required by the government concluded that major investment and reorganisation of services were required to meet the government's financial and other performance targets. A selection of comparative performance targets is shown in *Appendix B*. Organisations that consistently under-perform on these key targets will be subject to a government-instigated review.

The MGH Board initially drew up a "long list" of proposals for redevelopment. These proposals were evaluated firstly against the non-financial criteria listed below:

- provision of a locally available and accessible in-patient facility;
- critical mass of service provision to ensure adequate staff coverage and the ability to recruit and retain high quality staff;
- access to relevant treatments and therapies;
- expansion capability for future service development;
- minimum disruption to existing service provision;
- acceptability to other health providers in the locality.

On the basis of the outcome of this evaluation, the Board reduced the choice of proposals to three. As well as meeting the minimum requirements of the non-financial evaluation, these three proposals were considered to have the greatest potential to offer value for money. Whichever proposal is chosen, at least some of the finance for the capital costs must be sought from private sector providers probably as part of a "Build, Operate, Lease" arrangement.

The main features of the three proposals, their expected strategic benefits and practical constraints are discussed below. The expected effects on performance measures are shown in *Appendix B*.

Proposal 1

Main features

Build a completely new hospital on a new site that would provide the full range of services currently available within MGH (excluding very specialised procedures, as now). A suitable "brown-field" site has been identified just outside the main city centre, approximately two miles from the current hospital. The seller, Romstat Properties, has had difficulty selling this land because the planning authorities have consistently refused applications for housing development. The cost of this land is currently €10 million. The sale value of the land and buildings on the existing three sites is estimated as €25 million as their location is suitable for housing and / or commercial development.

Benefits

There would be a public sector full-service health provider in the district, which would meet with widespread support from the public, local health groups and politicians. There would also be economies of scale from single-site provision of services that would allow substantial improvement in many performance measures.

A government requirement is that major redevelopment projects that propose full-service provision, such as Proposal 1, should have a formal procedure in place for ongoing evaluation of the project after completion. Some, especially the Finance Director, consider this a benefit but others think it is a waste of time and money and that the money would be better spent directly on patient care.

Additional income would be provided by the government for the provision of services as a consequence of increased activity (that is, higher numbers of patients treated for comparable health complaints).

Constraints / concerns

Government approval is required for all capital investment projects over €70 million irrespective of how they are to be financed. When building costs are taken into account, this Proposal will almost certainly exceed this limit and the process of obtaining approval will inevitably introduce delays into the decision process.

A potential area of concern is the need to obtain planning permission from the local authority for the change of use of the three former hospital sites. The estimated sale value of these sites assumes they will be accompanied by planning permission for housing development. A representative from the local government office was invited along to discuss this issue with the Board and Board members have been given to understand that there would be no problems in obtaining the necessary permission, subject to an environmental audit. A firm of environmental consultants has been asked to prepare a detailed report on the likely environmental impacts of the proposed redevelopment.

Proposal 2

Main features

This Proposal would be to build a completely new hospital on a new site that would provide services only for acutely ill patients, out-patients and accident and emergency. Other services would be "de-merged" and possibly re-merged with other, similar units in neighbouring districts. Maternity and child welfare services could be merged with a neighbouring clinic on the other side of the city. Mental health services could be taken over by a private organisation that has for some years shown interest in such a venture, although the company does not wish to buy the land and buildings. MGH would therefore retain ownership of the land and buildings and lease them to the private provider for the duration of the contract, which is likely to be for an initial period of five years.

If this Proposal was selected, MGH would have no managerial responsibility for the operation of maternity, child welfare and mental health services although there would be some need for co-operation on referrals to and from the main hospital. The Romstat Properties' site would also be suitable for this Proposal, although it will be larger than necessary. The proceeds from land sales would be around €15 million, which is €10 million lower than with Proposal 1, as MGH would retain ownership of the land and buildings occupied by the privatised mental health service.

Benefits

This Proposal is likely to yield the greatest improvement in many performance measures, both managerial and clinical. It would also allow the Group to focus on "core" business. The maternity and child welfare services will benefit from greater specialisation – for example, with more patients, the enlarged organisation in the neighbouring district can employ more specialist staff on a full-time basis rather than, as at present, sharing specialist human resources.

The benefits to the mental health service are less obvious, other than freeing MGH management time.

There will be an increase in the volume of activity of comparable treatments, but a decrease in overall activity because of the de-merging of maternity and mental health. However, because treatments have widely varying costs, it is possible that income from activities will increase while the overall volume of activities decreases.

Constraints / concerns

This Proposal would cause some local opposition, although the Board believes it can manage the protests and political interference more successfully than ten years ago.

As noted above, the land identified for Proposal 1 is being considered for this Proposal also although there would be land to spare, at least for the foreseeable future. The Romstat Properties' board is unwilling to split the site into two or more lots so MGH must buy it all or look for another suitable site. A suggestion would be for MGH to buy the entire site and then sell the surplus land, if a buyer could be found at all given Romstat's difficulty in selling the entire site.

As with Proposal 1, government approval for the capital spend would be required.

The company secretary of MGH has informed the Board that although there are no major legislative issues that might affect the redevelopment, there is a minor concern in respect of the Human Rights Act because certain sections of the population would have to travel a short distance outside the region to obtain treatment. This is being investigated.

It is also apparent that some staff will no longer be required by MGH. The MGH Board believes these staff will be taken over by the acquiring providers and that there will be no serious opposition by the staff concerned and no severance costs for MGH.

Proposal 3

Main features

This is the "minimum" change Proposal. This would mean refurbishment of existing premises and some reorganisation and relocation of service provision. This Proposal barely meets the non-financial criteria but is included as a benchmark.

Benefits

The main benefit is that it is likely to be the lowest-cost Proposal and can be completed in the shortest time. Also, as it is below the government's capital cost approval level, the MGH Board could approve the expenditure and financing.

Constraints / concerns

This is considered the least favourable Proposal by the Board and most staff but is included to provide a benchmark against which the undoubted higher costs of the other two Proposals will be compared. However, if this "minimum" change Proposal is chosen, many clinical staff have indicated they will leave, causing a staffing crisis.

A major constraint on "rebuild" redevelopments is the need to maintain capacity while the renovations are taking place. This involves closing down sections of the hospital one at a time and transferring the activity to another part of the hospital or buying the required services from another health provider, either in the public or private sector. There will therefore be a substantial amount of upheaval and dual running costs for a period of time with this Proposal.

A further potential problem is that private providers of funds are likely to be less than enthusiastic about loaning this amount of money for what is mainly a refurbishment project, other than at an unacceptably high cost of finance over a relatively short (15 years) period of time. An alternative way of raising the money would be a combination of public appeal for funds and government grants. It is also possible some European Union funds would be available for some aspects of the renovation.

4. Selection criteria, short-listing and choice of contractor

4.1 Selection criteria

The MGH Board advertised for expressions of interest from building contractors and development consortia. All potential bidders were provided with information about the three Proposals under consideration. They were required to submit details about their organisation and any proposed sub-contractors, and also to demonstrate a proven ability to deliver on similar size contracts. At this stage they were not required to submit estimates of costs.

The selection process was done in two stages by a project planning team that consisted of staff from the finance and planning departments. The first stage was to review all bids to determine whether they met the six basic selection criteria listed below. The project planning team established these criteria, which were based on criteria used by similar organisations undertaking similar redevelopment reviews.

(i) An ability and willingness to contract for any of the three Proposals.

(ii) Evidence of sound contractual arrangements, existing or proposed, between the lead contractor and sub-contractors.

(iii) An ability to provide, or arrange, financing for the project although MGH Board is hopeful that the Zamorna government will provide some assistance with the capital costs.

(iv) An outline redevelopment plan including profiles of the management team and evidence that a suitably qualified workforce is available for design and construction.

(v) Statement of ability to observe the environmental and regulatory requirements of the chosen Proposal.

(vi) Statement of compliance with MGH's policies on equality and diversity.

4.2 Expressions of interest and short-listing

Twelve companies or consortia submitted expressions of interest. Ten companies or consortia were eliminated because they failed to meet adequately all the criteria. This has resulted in a short list of only two contractors who have now been asked to submit cost estimates for the three Proposals.

Contractor 1 – ArkFin Consortium

Fifteen companies are involved in this consortium as main or sub-contractors. The "lead contractor" is the main building firm, Arkwright plc, a UK-based construction company, whose shares are listed on a UK stock exchange. Its five-year financial summary is shown in *Appendix D*.

Arkwright plc has been established for over 50 years and has a sound financial history, apart from a three-year loss-making period some ten years ago. This was due to the company under-pricing its bids in order to win large public sector contracts. A shareholder revolt caused management changes and the company returned to profitability within two years.

Two non-executive Directors of MGH expressed concern about the short-listing of ArkFin. The consortium has been assembled specifically for the MGH contract and some of the participating firms have little or no experience of major health sector construction work. Also, Arkwright plc's contractual agreements with its sub-contractors were contained in a briefer document than the Board had expected. Arkwright plc's Chief Executive argued that the relationship with their sub-contractors was a commercial one and, as the lead contractor would hold ultimate responsibility for completion of the contract, the MGH Board did not need to concern itself with the details. As there were only two companies being short-listed, and to re-advertise for expressions of interest would involve an unacceptable delay to the start of the project, the NED's concern was over-ruled by the rest of the MGH Board.

Contractor 2 – LinMel Group

This is a US group that was originally a construction company but has now diversified into other areas, including providing financing for its larger projects. It has been working in Europe for some years on similar large-scale public sector projects with private finance involvement. It has a good reputation for delivering on time and within budget. The senior management team of LinMel believes the company can provide all the services necessary using its own companies but reserves the right to sub-contract if necessary. Its five-year financial summary is shown in *Appendix E*. Its shares are listed on a US stock exchange.

4.3 Submission of cost estimates

The two short-listed contractors were asked to submit outline cost estimates and finance terms for all three restructuring Proposals. Key information from the two bids is shown below.

Proposal 1 - Centralised services in new hospital

	ArkFin	*LinMel*
	€ million	*€ million*
Building costs (including costs of equipment and fittings)	115·00	105·00
Total finance required (net of proceeds from land sales – see *Note 1*)	100·00	90·00
Annual lease charge – see *Note 2*	7·82	9·37
Finance period	25 years	25 years
Estimated completion date (number of months from date of signing contract)	+36	+40

Note 1: This is the sum of:	*€ million*	*€ million*
Building costs	115·00	105·00
Cost of the Romstat Properties' land	10·00	10·00
Less estimated sale value of land and buildings of all three old sites	(25·00)	(25·00)

Note 2: The lease payments are for the provision of finance for the total capital cost of the redevelopment, that is €100 million (ArkFin) or €90 million (LinMel).

Proposal 2 – Centralisation of acute services in new hospital and de-merger of maternity, child welfare and mental health services.

	ArkFin	*LinMel*
	€ million	*€ million*
Building costs (including cost of equipment and fittings)	100·00	95·00
Total finance required (including net cost of land – see *Note 1*)	95·00	88·00
Annual lease charge – see *Note 2*	7·43	8·24
Finance period	25 years	25 years
Estimated completion date (number of months from date of signing contract)	+30	+35

Note 1: This is the sum of:	*€ million*	*€ million*
Building costs	100·00	93·00
Cost of the Romstat Properties' land	10·00	10·00
Less estimated sale value of land and buildings of old DH and MCWC sites	(15·00)	(15·00)

The cost may be reduced if MGH decides, and is able, to sell the portion of the Romstat Properties' land that would be surplus to immediate requirements with this Proposal.

Note 2: The lease payments are for the provision of finance for the total capital cost of the redevelopment, that is €95.0 million (ArkFin) or €88.0 million (LinMel).

Proposal 3 – "Minimum" proposal to refurbish and reorganise.

	ArkFin	*LinMel*
	€ million	*€ million*
Building costs (including structural work)	30·00	28·50
Annual cost of finance	3·05	2·90
Finance period	15 years	15 years
Estimated completion date (number of months from date of signing contract)	+36	+30

The following contractual obligations and conditions will be imposed by MGH on the winning contractor if Proposal 1 or 2 is chosen.

- MGH will start the lease payments only when the buildings and specified support services are available and performing to defined quality standards.
- The buildings will be maintained as part of the contract throughout the lease period. At the end of this period, the hospital group can acquire the buildings, renew the financing contract, or put it out to re-tender. These end-of-lease terms are still to be negotiated.
- Penalty deductions will be applied if the building and specified support services are not available or not performing to defined quality standards.

4.4 Choice of contractor

After some delays, the decision was to award the contract to ArkFin, despite its lack of experience with this type of contract, as its bid carried the lowest annual charges for Proposals 1 and 2 and its estimated completion dates for these two Proposals were shorter than LinMel's proposal. Its completion date for Proposal 3 is slightly longer than LinMel's but the MGH Board believes it is unlikely Proposal 3 will be the preferred choice.

The MGH Board called a special meeting to review the evaluation team's recommendation. Some of the Non-Executive Directors, especially Carlos Cluntz, were strongly opposed to the choice of ArkFin as the costs and completion dates suggested by the contractor appeared extremely optimistic. The costs factor in particular caused concern. As Mr Cluntz pointed out, it was not sensible to give the contract to the lowest-cost bidder if those costs were cut so fine they threatened the long-term survival of the contractor and its associates. However, the dissenting Non-Executive Directors were over-ruled by the overwhelming support given by the executives and the reluctant compliance of the other Non-Executive Directors.

4.5 Resignation of Non-Executive Director and launch of investigation

Two days after the special meeting to approve the award of the contract, Carlos Cluntz made a very public resignation. He stated his reasons as the "unjustifiable and unsupportable" choice of ArkFin. He very readily agreed to discuss the reasons for his resignation with local health groups, media and politicians. The resulting public outcry has led the government to send a senior health executive from a neighbouring region to conduct an investigation. This investigation is expected to take between six and eight weeks.

NOTE: Zamorna is not *the UK and the health system is* not *the UK's National Health Service (NHS).*

Appendices A, B, C, D, E and F follow

Demographic statistics for the region

	Actual as at 2003	*Forecast for 2013*
Population total	518,000	534,000
Percentage:	%	%
aged under 4	5·2	4·8
aged 5 - 16	12·5	11·7
aged 17 - 25	10·6	9·7
aged 26 - 45	26·3	24·3
aged 46 - 60	17·4	18·5
aged 61 - 80	20·3	22·5
aged over 80	7·7	8·5

The male / female split is roughly equal until the age bands 61 - 80 and over 80 when there is an increasingly higher percentage of women than men.

Population in 2003 by social category (to nearest 000)

Total population of working age	292
By category:	
Professional	18
Managerial / technical	90
Skilled	125
Semi skilled	46
Unskilled	13

Notes:

1. No forecast is available of future population by social category.

2. Unemployment in the region is 5·5% compared with the national average of 7·5%. It is mainly concentrated in the semi-skilled and unskilled categories. Unemployment in the other categories is typically of the "between jobs" type.

3. Unemployed people are included within the relevant social category.

Performance measures

	MGH	Average for comparative organisations	Expected outcomes (1st full year of activities)		
			Proposal 1	Proposal 2	Proposal 3
Hospital waiting times					
Out-patients:					
percentage of treatments completed within 3 months	68%	60%	75%	80%	72%
In-patients					
percentage of patients admitted within 3 months	65%	75%	78%	80%	70%
percentage of patients admitted within 12 months	95%	100%	100%	100%	100%
Complaints					
Number of complaints received and investigated	1,250	950	1,050	950	1,150
Number of complaints upheld	175	50	75	60	80
Number of staff complaints - all causes (harassment, unfair dismissal etc)	185	85	85	50	65
Financial					
Percentage under/(over) spend on cash limit	(5%)	0	0	0	0
Staff costs as percentage of total operating costs	75%	70%	73%	70%	75%
Average cost per out-patient treatment (excluding accident and emergency cases)	€ 850	€ 775	€775	€765	€825
Average cost per in-patient treatment (excluding maternity)	€1,450	€1,425	€1,550	€1,425	€1,550
Approx fixed/variable cost ratio	75/25	68/72	70/30	68/72	75/25

Note: Expected outcomes are at 2003 cost levels.

Financial statements of Mayah Group of Hospitals

Profit and loss account

	Note	For the year ended 2003	For the year ended 2002
		€000	€000
Income from activities	1	231,520	215,250
Other income	2	14,500	23,500
Expenses connected with activities		257,350	245,200
Surplus / (deficit) on activities		(11,330)	(6,450)
Profit / (loss) on disposal of assets		550	(365)
Surplus / (deficit) before interest		(10,780)	(6,815)
Interest receivable		650	425
Interest payable and other finance charges		(250)	(125)
Surplus / (deficit) for the year		(10,380)	(6,515)

Balance sheet

	Note	€000	€000	€000	€000
Fixed assets:					
Intangible			150		150
Tangible			132,655		135,260
Current assets:					
Stock		3,520		2,560	
Debtors	3	19,250		22,500	
Cash and short-term investments		780		250	
Total current assets			23,550		25,310
Current liabilities:					
Amounts due within 1 year			(25,025)		(19,500)
Total assets less current liabilities			131,330		141,220
Creditors falling due after 1 year			(650)		(560)
Provisions for liabilities			(2,350)		(1,950)
Total assets less liabilities			128,330		138,710
Financed by:					
Capital and reserves:					
Public capital	4		122,710		133,090
Revaluation reserve			3,520		3,520
Other reserves			2,100		2,100
Total capital and reserves			128,330		138,710

Notes

1. Income from activities is money provided by government, based on standard rates for the activities undertaken.
2. Other income is mainly from the treatment of private patients.
3. Debtors is mainly money owed by the government for treatments provided and from other hospitals whose patients have been treated by MGH. Money owed by private health insurers for patients treated privately is also included here.
4. Public capital is roughly the equivalent of shareholders' capital. Public capital plus reserves is the value of the organisation to its owners; that is the public.

Five-year financial summary for Arkwright plc

	2003 € million	2002 € million	2001 € million	2000 € million	1999 € million
Profit and loss account					
Group turnover	2,650·30	1,850·20	1,622·20	1,450·00	1,205·50
Group operating profit	247·50	195·20	175·20	125·00	95·50
Profit on disposal of fixed assets	5·60	12·50	65·00	-	6·50
Net interest payable	(35·20)	(25·00)	(22·50)	(19·50)	(19·80)
Profit before taxation	217·90	182·70	217·70	105·50	82·20
Taxation charge	(62·50)	(51·20)	(65·00)	(25·20)	(21·20)
Profit for the financial year	155·40	131·50	152·70	80·30	61·00
Dividends declared	(38·50)	(32·50)	(28·55)	(18·50)	(16·50)
Profit retained	116·90	99·00	124·15	61·80	44·50
Balance sheet					
Intangible assets – goodwill	171·85	-	-	-	-
Investment properties	465·00	465·00	449·50	187·30	175·00
Other fixed assets	225·00	179·50	145·00	132·70	98·50
Net current assets	935·50	705·55	595·00	438·50	345·20
Non-current creditors and provisions	(40·50)	(15·10)	(16·50)	(25·00)	(21·50)
Capital employed	1,756·85	1,334·95	1,173·00	733·50	597·20
Represented by:					
Called-up ordinary share capital	240·00	240·00	240·00	150·00	150·00
Share premium account	425·00	425·00	425·00	235·50	235·50
Revaluation reserve	161·00	161·00	108·05	94·40	72·20
Profit and loss account	480·85	363·95	264·95	140·80	79·00
Shareholders' funds	1,306·85	1,189·95	1,038·00	598·50	536·70
Long-term debt	450·00	145·00	135·00	110·00	95·00
	1,756·85	1,334·95	1,173·00	733·50	631·70
Statistics					
Number of shares in issue at year end (millions)	480·00	480.00	480.00	300·00	300·00
Basic earnings per share	0·32	0.27	0.32	0·27	0·20
Dividends per share	(0·08)	(0.07)	(0.06)	(0·06)	(0·06)
Shareholders' funds per share	2·72	2·48	2·16	2·00	1·79
Dividend cover (times)	4·04	4.05	5.35	4·34	3·70
Debt : debt + equity	25·61	10.86	11.51	18·40	15·04
Interest cover (times)	4·41	5.26	6.79	4·12	3·08
Profitability (profit before tax/turnover)	8·22%	9.87%	13.42%	7·28%	6·82%

Appendix E

Five-year financial summary for LinMel Inc

	2003	*2002*	*2001*	*2000*	*1999*
	$ million	*$ million*	*$ million*	*$ million*	*$ million*
Profit and loss account					
Group turnover	1,352·20	1,150·20	952·25	1,250·20	1,050·20
Group operating profit	235·00	184·03	142·84	225·04	178·53
Profit on disposal of fixed assets	0·00	0·00	25·30	0·00	0·00
Net interest payable	(28·00)	(28·00)	(22·50)	(22·50)	(22·50)
Profit before taxation	207·00	156·03	145·64	202·54	156·03
Taxation charge	53·82	40·57	37.87	52·66	40·57
Profit for the financial year	153·18	115·46	107.·7	149·88	115·47
Dividends declared	(105·20)	(46·19)	(43.·1)	(59·95)	(46·19)
Profit retained	47·98	69·28	64·66	89·93	69·28
Balance sheet					
Fixed assets	778·50	712·41	527·91	433·50	354·66
Intangible assets	52·50	50·00	50·00	45·00	45·00
Net current assets	192·87	216·16	227·46	237·43	228·62
Non-current creditors and provisions	(9·24)	(9·92)	(8·00)	(8·22)	(10·50)
Capital employed	1,014·63	968·65	797·37	707·71	617·78
Represented by:					
Called-up ordinary share capital	125·00	125·00	125·00	125·00	125·00
Share premium account	115·00	115·00	115·00	115·00	115·00
Revaluation reserve	25·00	25·00	25·00	0·00	0·00
Profit and loss account	399·63	351·65	282·37	217·71	127·78
Shareholders' funds	664·63	616·65	547·37	457·71	367·78
Long-term debt	350·00	350·00	250·00	250·00	250·00
	1,014·63	968·65	797·37	707·71	617·78
Statistics					
Number of shares in issue at year end (millions)	125·00	125·00	125·00	125·00	125·00
Basic earnings per share	1·23	0·92	0·86	1·20	0·92
Dividends per share	(0·84)	(0·37)	(0·34)	(0·48)	(0·37)
Shareholders' funds per share	5·32	4·93	4·38	3·66	2·94
Dividend cover (times)	1·46	2·50	2·50	2·50	2·50
Debt : debt + equity	34·50	36·21	31·35	35·33	40·47
Interest cover (times)	5·47	4·12	4·79	6·66	5·13
Profitability (profit before tax/turnover	15·31%	13·57%	15·29%	16·20%	14·86%

Note: The accounts of this US company are laid out in a similar form to those of Arkwright plc for ease of comparison.

Glossary of Terms

Acute hospital

A hospital that offers a wide range of medical and surgical services and procedures for both in-patients and out-patients. Usually also provides accident and emergency services.

Brown-field site

A site that has been built on previously and the old buildings demolished (as compared with a "green-field" site that has never been developed).

Build, Operate, Lease (BOL)

A type of lease arrangement whereby a company or consortium builds and services a facility and leases it to the client (in this case, MGH). Such a deal is usually over a very long period of time, typically 30+ years. Build, Operate, Lease arrangements typically incorporate aspects of both finance and operating leases. A finance lease is where the agreed term of the lease approximates the expected lifetime of the asset. These are often also termed *capital lease* or a *full pay out lease.* An operating lease is usually specific to the purchase of a specific type of equipment and typically there are break clauses in the contract, which can be cancelled much more easily than a finance lease. However, there are usually financial penalties for early termination.

Clinical staff

Staff employed to provide any form of medical or nursing treatment, including dentistry and midwifery.

Completed treatment

Successful or terminated treatment or series of treatments for the same complaint. Treatments may be terminated for a variety of reasons; for example patient chooses to discontinue treatment or treatment is having no beneficial effect.

Efficiency adjusted annual cost saving

The reduction in total costs of providing an equivalent number of comparable treatments (compared with the current organisational configuration) directly attributable to improvements in efficiency of service.

Full-time equivalent

Staff numbers are expressed in full-time equivalents, as MGH employs a number of part-time staff. For example, an employee who works half of the hours of a full-time employee is half a full-time equivalent.

Health provider

Any hospital, clinic or surgery, public or private, that provides any type of healthcare.

In-patient

Patients who are allocated a bed and stay in the hospital for at least eight hours for treatment. In-patients do not necessarily stay overnight.

Out-patient

Patients who have short consultations or series of consultations with clinical staff and do not require the allocation of a bed.

Treatment and treatment episode

Any medical or surgical procedure or series of procedures for the same complaint.

Mayah Group of Hospitals – Unseen material provided on examination day

Additional (unseen) information relating to the case is given on pages 19 – 23.

Read all of the additional material before you answer the question.

ANSWER THIS QUESTION – 100 MARKS

You are employed by Ross, Jackson and Broomes, the firm of professional advisers which is working with MGH. You have been seconded to the group to lead the project management team.

Write a report to the MGH Board in which you

- evaluate and prioritise the strategic issues facing MGH at the present time;
- evaluate the three redevelopment Proposals;
- recommend actions for addressing the strategic issues, including the most appropriate redevelopment Proposal.

Note: The assessment matrix, which your script will be marked against, is on the next page for your reference.

CIMA

November 2004 – Assessment Matrix for Case Study – Mayah Group of Hospitals

	Criterion	Marks*	Clear Pass	Pass	Marginal Pass	Marginal Fail	Fail	Clear Fail
Process	**Prioritisation (of issues)**	20	Clearly prioritised in a logical order and based on a clear rationale. 17-20	Issues prioritised with justification. 11-16	Evidence of issues being listed in order of importance, but rationale unclear. 10	Issues apparently in priority order, but without a logical justification or rationale. 8-9	Little attempt at prioritisation or justification or rationale. 4-7	No attempt at prioritisation or justification. 0-3
Process	**Knowledge**	10	Thorough display of relevant technical knowledge at an appropriate level. 9-10	Some display of relevant knowledge at an appropriate level. 6-8	Identification of some relevant knowledge, but largely lacking in depth. 5	Knowledge displayed without clear application. Some sections appear unreferenced. 3-4	Some knowledge displayed, but little attempt to justify it or use it in context. 1-2	Little evidence of knowledge displayed. Fundamental misconceptions. 0
Process	**Numerical skills**	15	Relevant data clearly identified. Calculations correct. Workings clearly shown. 13-15	A few relatively minor technical inaccuracies. Calculations mainly clear and logical. 9-12	Some results not supported by workings. Occasional errors. Some calculations avoided. 8	Some inappropriate or incorrect analysis carried out. Frequent errors or omissions. 6-7	Little analysis offered. Calculations often unclear or irrelevant. Workings incomprehensible. 3-5	A general absence of calculation or analysis, or calculations incorrect and often misleading. 0-2
Presentation	**Structure (recommend-ations)**	20	Good evaluation of options. Conclusions stated clearly with valid recommendations. 17-20	Fair evaluation of alternatives. Some recommendations omitted. 11-16	Limited evaluation of alternatives, or poorly supported recommendations. 10	Very few alternatives evaluated and with unsupported recommendations. 8-9	Little consideration of alternatives. Few or no conclusions. Unclear recommendations. 4-7	No identification of alternatives and no recommendations offered. 0-3
Presentation	**Business communication**	5	Excellent and appropriate communication in good business style. Messages clear and effective. 5	Good communication skills, with occasional lack of clarity and some weaknesses in style. 4	Some lack of clarity in communication and understandability. General business style is weak. 3	Business style is weak and, in general, answer is poorly conveyed. 2	Use of language ineffective; communication generally poor. Of little use to recipient. 1	Lack of evidence of suitable language and failure to communicate ideas. 0
Presentation	**Format**	5	Precise professional format and structure, with good use of relevant appendices. 5	Clear and recognisable format with a logical structure. 4	Recognisable format and structure, although occasionally unclear. Limited use of appendices. 3	Recognisable format but poor use of structure. Difficult to navigate. 2	Little attempt to use the appropriate format. Little attempt to structure content. 1	No attempt made to use appropriate format. Content unstructured. 0
Overall	**Business awareness**	5	High level of business awareness and appropriate use of real-world examples. 5	Good business awareness and use of real-world examples. 4	Some business awareness shown, plus occasional use of real-world examples. 3	A general lack of business awareness shown. Some use of real-world examples, occasionally unrealistic or irrelevant. 2	Little business awareness evident. Very few real-world examples, some clearly unrealistic or irrelevant. 1	No business awareness evident and no obvious attempt to use real-world examples. 0
Overall	**Breadth**	10	Most key issues identified, covering a range of views. 9-10	A number of key issues identified, covering a slightly narrower range of views. 6-8	A few important issues identified, expressing a fairly limited point of view. 5	Several important issues omitted, or too many issues considered. 3-4	Many important issues omitted, or a series of diverse points made. 1-2	Very few issues considered, or a long list of points covered. 0
Overall	**Depth**	10	Each issue covered to an appropriate level of detail. Answer is comprehensive and evidences critical thinking. 9-10	Several issues covered to an appropriate level of detail. Some evidence of analysis and critical thinking. 6-8	A number of key issues raised, although occasionally lacking detailed analysis. 5	Several important issues lacked the level of analysis required. 3-4	Only very brief analysis of the issues identified. 1-2	Little or no attempt to analyse the issues identified. 0
	TOTAL	100						

***Note** The number of available marks allocated to each criterion may vary from paper to paper. A criterion could have a minimum mark of 5 and a maximum mark of 20.

Mayah Group of Hospitals – Unseen material provided on examination day

Read this information before you answer the question

Note: a reminder of the abbreviations used, for your reference:

DH = the district hospital

MH = the mental hospital

MCWC = the maternity and child welfare clinic

Results of investigation

The senior health executive from a neighbouring region sent in to investigate the allegations made by a Non-Executive Director (Carlos Cluntz) of misconduct in the awarding of the redevelopment contract (the "Investigating Executive") has completed his investigation and delivered three main conclusions:

1. There were a number of irregularities in the process of selecting the contractor.
2. Carlos Cluntz's contention that there were serious managerial weaknesses in the MGH Board was upheld. In particular, the investigating executive discovered that John Asta, the Chief Executive, was a shareholder in Romstat Properties. Although there was no evidence that he had attempted to influence the purchase terms of the Romstat land, he was required by his contract of service to declare such interests. The investigation also revealed that a Non-Executive Director, John Vance, undertakes freelance consulting work for MGH which he has not declared at Board meetings when contracts for the provision of such services have been discussed and awarded.
3. Although there were documents detailing MGH's corporate governance policy and procedures and the Chief Executive had ultimate responsibility, there was no supporting managerial or administrative framework to ensure the policy was followed and monitored.

The main recommendation from the Investigating Executive is that MGH needs to strengthen and improve its management structure.

A second recommendation was made that strategies for MGH achieving its objectives must recognise a wide range of issues, including ethical considerations.

As a result of the Investigating Executive's critical report, the Chairman, Chief Executive, Finance Director and John Vance have resigned. The Vice Chairman, who has recovered from her period of ill health, has been appointed Acting Chairman. Temporary appointments have also been made to the positions of Chief Executive and Director of Finance. The Acting Chairman, with the approval of her Board, has invited Carlos Cluntz back onto the Board as Non-Executive Director. He has accepted. This still leaves a vacancy for a Non-Executive Director. No one has yet been appointed.

The Investigating Executive criticised ArkFin for "inappropriate" discussions with some of the outgoing MGH Directors during the original bidding process but stopped short of claiming that ArkFin had done anything illegal or unethical. Its selection as "preferred building contractor" was therefore allowed to stand, subject to the following criteria:

- acceptance of its detailed cost estimates;
- that the *financing* of the contract be re-opened to limited competitive tender by at least one other company.

Appointment of advisers

As a result of this investigation, the new Board has appointed a firm of professional advisers, Ross, Jackson and Broomes, to assist with re-evaluating the choice of lead contractor and evaluating the restructuring Proposals. This advisory firm specialises in public sector consultancy work of this kind and is very experienced, if expensive. Ross, Jackson and Broomes will lead a Project Evaluation Team that will include representatives from managerial, administrative and clinical departments in MGH. Its terms of reference are:

- to evaluate and prioritise the strategic issues facing MGH at the present time;
- to evaluate the three redevelopment Proposals;
- to recommend actions for addressing the strategic issues, including the most appropriate redevelopment Proposal.

Projected overspend

ArkFin has now submitted detailed cost estimates for building and financing the three redevelopment Proposals. The totals are shown in *Table 1* (below) along with other forecast information prepared by the Project Evaluation Team. The costs of the project if Proposal 1 or 2 is chosen are likely to be much higher than originally expected and the project would take much longer to complete. The main reasons for these changes have been identified as:

- Land prices have increased since the outline bid was submitted and Romstat Properties believes that new planning laws mean the company might now be able to obtain permission for the site to be developed for limited commercial use. The Romstat land now has an estimated market value of €25 million. However, the estimated sale value of the land and buildings on the existing sites has also increased.
- Surveys of the proposed Romstat Properties' site have discovered geological faults that were not evident at the time of the initial bid. This will make the building work more difficult and more expensive.
- The environmental study has resulted in requirements for a number of costly changes to the original building design. The local authority has indicated this work will be required as a condition of planning permission being given. This also will introduce a delay into the timescale for completion.

Table 1

	Note	Proposal 1	Proposal 2	Proposal 3
Cost of Romstat land *(€ million)*		25·00	25·00	0
Building costs *(€ million)*		145·00	115·00	35·00
Less: estimated sale proceeds of old land and buildings *(€ million)*	*1*	(30·00)	(24·00)	0
Net capital costs *(€ million)*	2	140·00	116·00	35·00
ArkFin's annual lease charge *(€ million)*		13·12	10·87	4·87
Duration of lease		25 years	25 years	15 years
Estimated completion date (months from date of signing contract)		+40 months	+36 months	+32 months
Forecast increase in activity	*3*	13·6%	21·4%	4·20%
Required income per annum *(€ million)*	*4*	266·25	246·00	253·31
Efficiency adjusted annual cost saving *(€ million)*	*5*	7·76	8·32	2·51

Notes

1. The Project Evaluation Team commissioned an independent valuer to value the land and buildings. With Proposal 1 the land and buildings of all three sites would be sold, although the value is almost exclusively for the land, as the buildings have virtually no alternative use other than as hospitals. With Proposal 2, only the MH and MCWC land and buildings would be sold.

The proceeds from the sale of the surplus Romstat Properties' land that would be available with Proposal 2 has now been estimated at €8 million. This estimate assumes planning permission for housing is received. This amount is excluded from the figures above, as it is so uncertain.

2. The Zamorna government has told MGH it can expect no financial assistance with capital expenditure for the investment required for redevelopment, which must now all be raised from private sector funding.

3. Increase in activity is, broadly, an increase in the number of patients treated for comparable health complaints. The required annual income reflects this increase in activity.

4. The government has indicated it will provide additional annual income required as a consequence of the redevelopment provided there is a "substantial" improvement in MGH's performance on patient-related performance measures. To date, it has not been more specific about the level of improvements required and has not seen the figures in *Table 1* or any supporting documents. The Project Evaluation Team has incorporated forecast lease charges into the required annual income.

5. Government targets require efficiency-adjusted cost improvements to be a minimum of 3% of annual income on major redevelopment projects and 1% on rebuild or refurbishment projects. These efficiency gains are reflected in the required annual income.

Competitive tender for the provision of finance

As required by the independent investigator, the MGH Board approached two companies for a competitive tender for financing the project. One was LinMel, which had bid for the original contract. The other was a subsidiary of an international bank. LinMel informed the Board they did not wish to tender. The bank submitted the following lease terms:

	Proposal 1	*Proposal 2*	*Proposal 3*
Annual lease charge (€ million)	15·42	12·78	4·60
Duration of lease	25 years	25 years	15 years

Methods of appraisal and evaluation of Proposals

The decision process in choosing the most favourable Proposal will involve expressing MGH's requirements in output terms. In other words, what outcomes would it be getting for the money invested. The following key variables will be considered as part of the appraisal and evaluation process. Each of the variables has been ranked on a scale of 1 to 3 (where 1 = best and 3 = worst) and weighted according to its relative importance. The resulting weighted scores have been determined by the project evaluation team but are in line with the government's guidelines.

		Proposal 1		*Proposal 2*		*Proposal 3*	
Variable	*Weighting*	*Rank*	*Weighted score*	*Rank*	*Weighted score*	*Rank*	*Weighted score*
Capital cost	0·10	3	0·30	2	0·20	1	0·10
Annual funding requirement	0·20	3	0·60	2	0·40	1	0·20
Reduction in cost per treatment	0·22	2	0·44	1	0·22	3	0·66
Increase in activity	0·25	2	0·50	1	0·25	3	0·75
Reduction in complaints received and investigated	0·05	2	0·10	1	0·05	3	0·15
Improvement in quality of patient care, as measured by reduced waiting times for treatment	0·18	2	0·36	1	0·18	3	0·54
Totals	1·00		2·30		1·30		2·40

These are not the only variables that will be considered in the evaluation process, but they are the ones most easily quantifiable. Also to be considered is how each Proposal will contribute to the achievement of MGH's four aims and how they will help address the strategic issues facing MGH at the present time.

Public sector organisations in Zamorna are required to show a 5% return on investment (that is, they use a discount rate of 5% to evaluate cash flows).

Operating and financing the project

In addition to the construction of the new buildings, ArkFin will provide building and equipment maintenance and replacement services as required by the terms of bidding. The costs of these services are included in the lease charge. Discussions are taking place with ArkFin about the consortium also providing ancillary services such as catering, laundry and cleaning services. If ArkFin is given the contract for these services, it will have a favourable effect on the terms of finance for the land and construction. The annual lease charge for Proposals 1 and 2 would reduce to €12·57 and €10·40 respectively. The charge for Proposal 3 would be unaffected.

The required annual income from government, shown above, has included an estimate of costs for ancillary services. The difference in costs between ArkFin providing the services and MGH continuing to provide them in-house is minimal. The possible differences in the quality of the services are difficult to quantify, although there are strong and differing views about this issue among the management and staff of MGH. At present MGH uses local suppliers for most of its consumables. It would probably lose this business if ArkFin took over the ancillary services. The main benefit of using ArkFin is in the favourable lease finance terms.

Demographic changes

A new demographic forecast has just been produced which is likely to have an impact on the future requirements of hospital services. This forecast shows a likely increase in the average age of the local population, and declining birth rate, due to its popularity as a retirement area. Many younger people are moving to other districts or regions. The revised forecast is shown below. These effects have not as yet been quantified or the effect on the hospitals in the group assessed.

	Actual as at 2003	*Original demographic forecast for 2013*	*Revised demographic forecast for 2013*
Population total	518,000	534,000	519,000
Percentage:	%	%	%
aged under 4	5·2	4·8	4·7
aged 5 - 16	12·5	11·7	11·4
aged 17 - 25	10·6	9·7	9·7
aged 26 - 45	26·3	24·3	22·5
aged 46 - 60	17·4	18·5	18·6
aged 61 - 80	20·3	22·5	24·3
aged over 80	7·7	8·5	8·8

The above information was provided in the pre-seen material

CIMA

Case Writer's Answer for Management Accounting – Case Study

MAYAH GROUP OF HOSPITALS

Report to: The Board of Mayah Group of Hospitals

From: Lead Consultant, Ross Jackson and Broomes

Date: 25 November 2004

Subject: Evaluation of the Strategic Issues facing MGH and Recommendations

REPORT CONTENT

Main sections

Appendices

1 INTRODUCTION

The Mayah Group of Hospitals (MGH) has suffered in recent years from poor and declining performance in many important areas of its operations. The reasons were identified as:

- the cost and inefficiency of operating over three sites;
- poor service delivery, as measured by established performance measures and compared with the national averages for comparative organisations;
- a general level of dissatisfaction of staff and high staff turnover;
- the changing health needs of the local population.

Following a strategic review of its operations the MGH board concluded that major investment and reorganisation of services were required. A "long list" of proposals for change was developed and evaluated, resulting in a short list of three proposals for change.

In summary, these are:

1. Provision of a full range of services in a new-build hospital;

2. Provision of selected services in a new-build hospital with de-merger of midwifery, child welfare and mental health services;

3. Refurbish and reorganise – a "minimum change" proposal.

A consortium has already been selected to undertake the redevelopment once the most appropriate proposal has been chosen, subject to the approval of final estimates of cost and time to completion. Following the resignation of a non-executive director, this selection was subject to scrutiny of an independent investigation by a senior health executive from a neighbouring region. This investigation allowed the choice of contractor to stand but led to the resignation of a number of executive and non-executive directors. The vacancies have been filled by permanent or temporary appointments.

As a consequence of the investigation and the major board upheavals, RJB was appointed to head a project evaluation team, which includes representatives from managerial, administrative and clinical areas of MGH's operations. The terms of reference and the aims of this report are discussed in the following section of the report.

2.0 TERMS OF REFERENCE, AIMS AND CONTENT OF THE REPORT AND ACKNOWLEDGEMENTS

2.1 Terms of reference

The terms of reference for the project were:

- To evaluate and prioritise the strategic issues facing MGH at the present time;
- To evaluate the three redevelopment proposals;
- To recommend actions for addressing the strategic issues, including the most appropriate redevelopment proposal.

2.2 Aims and content of report

The report has been produced by the RJB/MGH evaluation team in accordance with the terms of reference outlined above and following extensive consultations with staff and, where necessary and appropriate, outside experts. It aims to inform the MGH Board of the results of our evaluation and provide the required recommendations.

This report proceeds as follows. In section 3 we discuss the strategic issues currently facing MGH and our suggestions for manageing those issues. In section 4 the strengths, weaknesses, opportunities and threats of the three redevelopment proposals are evaluated together with an assessment of how each of the three proposals might contribute to the achievement of each of MGH's four objectives. In section 5 we present our recommendations.

2.3 Acknowledgements

The evaluation team wishes to acknowledge the advice, information and assistance given to it by staff and associates of MGH. Without their help the production of this report would not have been possible.

3 STRATEGIC ISSUES FACING MGH

3.1 Review of corporate aims

Before examining the strategic issues facing MGH, the project evaluation team considered the Group's aims. These are stated in the latest Annual Report and Accounts as:

- To deliver high quality health care to the residents of the region in which MGH operates;
- To provide value for money in terms of output per Euro spent;
- To improve the health of the local population by the use of pro-active measures;
- To recognise the needs of all the organisation's stakeholders and treat them with equal respect.

With the exception of "value for money", they are difficult to measure or quantify and even value for money has an element of subjectivity. However, they are similar to those of other comparable organisations and a re-examination of aims or overall objectives was not included in our terms of reference. We have therefore evaluated strategic issues in the context of the current aims, assuming their continuity.

Although all the issues discussed here are considered to be important, they have been prioritised in accordance with the informed opinion of the PET.

3.2 Evaluate and Prioritise Strategic Issues

3.2.1 Serious weaknesses in the management

These weaknesses have been manifest by poor performance on a range of measures and a weak board that has allowed serious concerns to be ignored. The composition of the board is also questionable; there is no clinician and there has been a vacancy for a NED for some time. These are basic governance issues that should have been addressed by the Chair and Chief Executive.

The recent report by an independent investigator has led to the resignations of some directors, but unless further action is taken in the immediate future, the governance problems will continue. The current Chair is in an acting capacity and only temporary appointments have been made to the positions of Chief Executive and Director of Finance. There is a vacancy for a non-executive director.

3.2.2 Financial performance

The financial position of MGH has deteriorated over the last year. From appendix C (in the pre-seen) it is noted that the deficit from last year of €6·515 million has increased to €10·380 million in the current year. This has been partly attributed to the costs of operating from three sites.

Of potential concern is the significant drop in "other income" down from €23·5 million to only €14·5 million despite a relatively affluent and ageing local population.

Using the Zamorna government's target return of a 5% return on investment, MGH should have achieved a surplus for the current year of €6·416 million on a capital and reserves balance of €128·330 million at the end of the current year.

3.2.3 Government targets and performance measures

The financial position has already been commented on in section 3.2.2. However there are also a number of important non-financial performance concerns as highlighted by appendix B (in the pre-seen). In terms of waiting times and complaints, MGH is only better then comparative organisations on one statistic – the percentage of treatments completed within three months. MGH needs to improve these performance measures in order to meet the Zamorna government's targets. Page 2 (pre-seen) states that not only are many of MGH's performance measures worse than comparable organisations, in many areas of service its performance is declining.

The consequences of these failures are that:

- Funding will be withheld;
- Patients will complain because of MGH's falling position in league tables relative to other comparative organisations;
- Recruitment will be even more difficult because staff will choose to work for better performing organisations.

3.2.4 Poor, outdated buildings and facilities
There is clearly a need for more modern facilities. This particular issue is being addressed by the redevelopment programme and is discussed further in section 5 of this report.

3.2.5 Resource limitations: staff and money
In any organisation or system where services are free at the point of delivery, demand will always exceed supply. Health services have additional strains as they are politically sensitive and new treatments and procedures increase patient/client expectations and put increasing pressures on limited resources.

This problem of demand exceeding supply is both a resource and ethical issue. There are two resource constraints, staff and money. There is a shortage of qualified staff, which has a direct impact on quality of health care, and government funding is never sufficient to meet all demands. This raises the ethical issues of "rationing" and prioritising patients and treatments. This issue is beyond the scope of the current evaluation.

3.2.6 Marketing/PR issues
Marketing in the public sector has a different meaning from in the private sector. To some extent, it is more akin to PR. The image of MGH is currently poor, and falling. Patients will choose to go to private hospitals if they can afford it, which means only the most disadvantaged patients, who are usually the ones with most ill health, will be treated by MGH. This creates a downward spiral, worse health outcomes means poorer performance on many measures. This may be happening already, as evidenced by the decline in "other income".

There is also evidence that people will move house to a different region if that region has better health facilities and outcomes, as measured by government targets. It is not proven, but possible, that the reasons for the demographic changes are related to the provision of health care in the region.

3.2.7 Balancing the needs of the various stakeholder groups.
There is a diverse range of stakeholder interests in any health organisation, and many will fit into more than one category so may have conflicting needs within themselves. For example, most patients will be taxpayers and all taxpayers will at some time be patients.

The main groups can be identified as:

- Government and local politicians, whose main aim is value for money and gaining electoral support through improved services.
- Patients, who want high quality services delivered on time in convenient locations but do not necessarily want to pay the appropriate rate for them.
- Staff and non-salaried associates, who want adequate salaries and good working conditions but also recognition for their contribution to health.
- Suppliers, who want to be paid on time but also have continuity of contractual relationships.

- Local community, who – like patients – want a good quality health service within reach but not always at their backdoor, the "NIMBY" argument.

- Taxpayers of Zamorna, who want value for money. There are diverse opinions in this group, for example some want good quality services and are prepared to pay more tax to get them, others do not want any tax increases but still want the services. This is the nature of the public sector.

Policies in relation to corporate governance, the awarding of contracts, and ethical issues need to be strengthened to ensure appropriate consideration of the needs of the stakeholder groups. A procedure for ensuring compliance needs to be put in place. These are necessary in order to meet the three main conclusions of the Investigating Executive (in the un-seen).

3.2.8 Demographic changes

The population of MGH's catchment region is ageing. This also will have an effect on health and performance measures. There has as yet been no attempt to determine the implications for this, but on the latest forecasts the region will have around 21,000 more residents over the age of 61 and around 13,000 fewer residents under 26. The current proposal to demerge maternity and child welfare does not appear to have considered these revised figures.

3.3 Use of balanced scorecard approach to evaluation of strategic issues

Many organisations in both the public and private sectors are using the balanced scorecard approach to translate their objectives and strategies into a "comprehensive set of performance measures that provide the framework for a strategic measurement and management system" (Kaplan and Norton 1986). Although this approach is not a panacea for poor judgment and management, it is a very useful tool that we are recommending MGH considers adopting. In this section of the report we discuss, briefly, what a balanced scorecard means in general and in the context of MGH.

The balanced score card approach to performance management specifically links performance measures to the strategic direction of an organisation. It is a multi-dimensional framework that utilises measurement as a means of describing an organisation's strategy. In essence the BSC aims to clarify an organisation's vision and strategy and translate them into tangible objectives and measures, which are selected because of their significance as drivers of future financial performance.

The BSC framework typically addresses four perspectives, normally defined as: (1) financial, (2) customer, (3) internal business processes, and (4) learning/growth. Each of these 4 perspectives, or quadrants, of the BSC will have a main aim, the achievement of which the chosen targets are expected to address. MGH has four objectives that can broadly be described as aims, which can then be attributed to each of the four quadrants of the BSC without too much difficulty. These are summarised in Appendix C. We have identified which of the current performance measures could be attributable to each quadrant and made some preliminary suggestions about additional measures that could be adopted.

EVALUATION OF REDEVELOPMENT PROPOSALS

Note: There are a large number of assumptions made in the following evaluation and many different approaches are available and valid.

4.1 Effect of redevelopment proposals on MGH's surplus/deficit

A financial summary showing the effect on MGH's surplus or deficit for the three proposals are shown in table 1 below. The supporting calculations and assumptions are to be found in appendix A at the end of this report.

TABLE 1

	Proposal 1 *€ (m)*	*Proposal 2* *€ (m)*	*Proposal 3* *€ (m)*
Surplus/(deficit) before interest and lease costs	26·401	17·220	10·268
Lowest lease charges (1)	13·120	10·870	4·600
Surplus/(deficit) for the year (2)	12·281	6·350	5·668

Notes:

1. Lease charges are for the ArkFin for proposals 1 and 2 assuming ArkFin also supplies ancillary services. The International bank's quotation has been used for proposal 3, as this is lower than ArkFin.

2. These figures ignore any gains there may be from disposal of land for proposals 1 and 2. In the case of proposal 1, there would be net cash receipts of €5 million over the 40-month build period (that is €25 million cost of Romstat land to be purchased, offset by the eventual sale of existing land for €30 million). In the case of proposal 2, there could be net cash receipts of €7 million over the 36-month build period (that is €25 million cost of land less €24 million sale of existing land and less €8 million estimates sale of surplus Romstat land).

These figures show that in the immediate future proposal 1 offers the most positive impact on MGH's surplus.

In terms of efficiency gains, only proposals 2 and 3 meet the government's targets in percentage terms (a minimum of 3% of annual income on major redevelopment projects and 1% on rebuild or refurbishment), as shown in table 2 below.

TABLE 2

	Proposal 1	*Proposal 2*	*Proposal 3*
Annual Income €m	266·250	246·000	253·310
Efficiency gains €m	7·76	8·32	2·51
Efficiency gains % per annum	2·91	3·38	0·99

4.2 Investment appraisal of redevelopment proposals

Public sector organisations in Zamorna are required to show a 5% return on investment. An NPV analysis on each investment was performed, in the first instance simply using MGH's "cost of capital". The key figures are shown in table 3 below. The detailed calculations are shown in appendix B.

TABLE 3

	Proposal 1 *€ (m)*	*Proposal 2* *€ (m)*	*Proposal 3* *€ (m)*
NPV before lease costs	11·10	110·94	-1·22
NPV after lease costs (including the ancillary services)	-141·94	-15·68	-42·46

After lease costs none of the proposals show a positive NPV. However, the government would not be providing finance at commercial rates, so decisions are more appropriately made on the pre-lease cost calculations. Other considerations are:

- The figures are provisional and forecasting so far into the future is subject to inaccuracies;
- The order of preference of the proposals is likely to stay the same.

We subsequently reviewed each of the proposals against the given criteria and the weighted scores already established, which were (in total)

	Proposal 1	*Proposal 2*	*Proposal 3*
Totals	2·30	1·30	2·40

However, this method does mix ranking absolute measures, such as capital cost and annual funding requirement, with relative measures such as a reduction in cost per treatment and increase in overall activity.

It is also useful to look at the percentage improvement in each measure, by proposal, against the current situation and against competitors. The figures are summarised in Appendix D. This shows that on a percentage basis proposal 2 shows the greatest improvement on all measures, except the waiting period for in-patients within 12 months, where the improvement ranks equally with proposals 1 and 3.

As we are required to assess the outcomes of the investment, it is necessary to use this initial exercise as the basis on which to build a more reasoned evaluation, taking into account other issues that are associated with each proposal.

We used a SWOT analysis framework to discuss the proposals. We have also evaluated each proposal in the context of the strategic issues identified and discussed in section 3.

The second part of our evaluation assesses the contribution of each proposal to the Group's objectives.

4.3 Strengths, weaknesses, opportunities and threats

Proposal 1

Strengths

This proposal aims to continue to provide a full service delivery of treatments and care but in modern buildings with better equipment. Main strengths are:

- It is likely to be the most favoured proposal by staff and the local population as it maintains the status quo but to a much higher standard than at present;
- Additional income from government can be expected to cover the additional activities; indeed this proposal demonstrates the highest annual surplus in the short term;
- All the performance measures detailed in Appendix B of the pre-seen will be improved;
- It will help MGH meet its main corporate aims, but to a lesser extent than proposal 2.

Weaknesses/threats
The key weakness is its lack of strategic focus. Modern health care facilities rarely combine such disparate activities as mental health, accident and emergency and maternity services. This lack of strategic focus is evident by the poorer performance forecast of most activity and efficiency measures when compared to Proposal 2. Other weaknesses are:

- It has the most expensive build costs at €145 million;
- It has a lower NPV than proposal 2;
- It has the longest completion date at 40 months, which introduces the potential threats of delays and budget over-runs.

An additional threat, which is also present in proposal 2, is the terms of the lease. The discount rates implied by ArkFin in their proposals are as follows:

	Excluding ancillary services % per annum		*Including ancillary services % per annum*	
	ArkFin	*International Bank*	*ArkFin*	*International Bank*
Proposal 1	8·0	10	7·5	Not available
Proposal 2	8·0	10	7·5	Not available
Proposal 3	11·0	10	9·0	Not available

The ArkFin rates seem very low compared with the international bank on proposals 1 and 2. However, as some of the NED's commented at the time ArkFin was approved by the MGH board, it is in no-one's interest for the terms of the contract to be so low the survival of the contractor is threatened.

ArkFin's latest quote for proposal 3 is much higher than both its original quote and that of than the international bank. This suggests the consortium is not interested in financing this type of refurbishment project.

Opportunities
There are two identifiable opportunities associated with "state of the art" facilities:

- The ability to attract and retain high quality staff;
- The ability to bid for additional funding from government and the private sector, for research as well as treatments. If this additional money were to be estimated and factored into the NPV analysis, the results might be more favorable.

Proposal 2

Strengths
This proposal should meet the same standards of care as proposal 1, but on selected services. Its main strength is financial – it has by far the most favourable outcome on the NPV analysis and demonstrates the greatest improvement on almost all performance measures in percentage terms. It still shows a negative NPV when lease costs are considered and this is discussed further in the recommendations section.

Another major strength is that it should allow greater specialisations of services across the region – not just in its own new hospital, but also in the "de-merged" maternity, child welfare and mental health services. It also shows the greatest improvement in some activity measures and at lower cost. This proposal has the lowest (therefore best) total weighted score. It ranks highest of the three proposals on the activity measures (reduction in cost per treatment, increase in activity and reduction in complaints). However, this is inevitable given that two of its main services are being de-merged.

Weaknesses/threats
The main weakness is the fact that it does not provide a full range of services. This is not a weakness from strategic, organisational or clinical perspectives but raises a potential threat, which is opposition from local population and health groups. Such opposition may cause extensive delays if, for example, the government orders a review.

Other threats with this proposal are:

- Surplus land which may be unsaleable;
- The value of the old land is less than expected, for example planning permission is not received and a buyer cannot be found. The converse of this is the opportunity it presents if planning permission is received and the land proves to be worth more than expected;
- The terms of the lease, as discussed under proposal 1;
- Some staff will no longer be required by MGH. They may well be offered employment by the acquiring providers, as suggested by the MGH Board, but there may be issues of redundancy or early retirement. This is a risk that should be costed and factored in to the evaluation.

Opportunities
These are likely to be similar to those with proposal 1, that is:

- The ability to attract and retain high quality staff;
- The ability to bid for additional funding from government and the private sector, for research as well as treatments. If this additional money were to be estimated and factored into the NPV analysis, the results might be more favourable.

Proposal 3

Strengths
This proposal's main strengths are:

- lowest overall cost in terms of both capital and revenue requirement;
- It has the shortest completion date at +32 months;
- It provides for a surplus in the immediate future, although less than the other two proposals;
- It maintains a full service provision;
- All performance measures would be improved, although to a lesser extent than is generally the case with the other two proposals;
- No ongoing evaluation will be required to satisfy the government.

Weaknesses
The weaknesses are:

- It does not provide a positive NPV. Also, the evaluation does not take into account the probability that further renovations and redevelopment will be necessary within the next 25-28 years – to a much greater extent than with proposals 1 or 2;
- Many performance measures continue to be below comparative organisations;

- It continues to use old buildings. The problems associated with this are unlikely to be completely overcome by refurbishment;
- Health services for the region would continue to be provided over more than one site;
- There would be significant adverse impact on patients during the build period because of upheaval on the present main site;
- It is a "sticking plaster" solution that will almost certainly only delay the inevitable and, in the long term, result in higher total costs;
- Apart from creating a financial surplus in the year this proposal would appear to conflict with some of MGH's main aims, and in particular the need to consider all the organisation's stakeholders.

Threats

- The staff discontent is the greatest threat, as many may leave and recruiting new staff of sufficiently high calibre may prove difficult;
- Providers of funds are not enthusiastic about financing refurbishment projects. It may prove difficult to find financing at all if this proposal is chosen.

Opportunities

There are no opportunities that can be identified with this proposal, other than the – possible – opportunity cost of the money saved. If the money saved on buildings can be spent on more and better equipment, to the benefit of patients, then the potential staffing crisis may be overcome. However, it is unlikely that new and more equipment will compensate for remaining in antiquated buildings.

4.4 Assessment of contribution to Group objectives

A summary of the development proposals is shown below:

Objective 1 – Delivering High Quality Health Care

As a strategy to assist MGH meet its objectives, proposal 1 contributes directly to this first objective. It clearly aims to deliver high quality health care to the residents of the region, although the quality of care is likely to be as high with proposal 2. Proposal 3 is unlikely to deliver the same quality of service, whatever amount is spent on equipment.

Objective 2 – Value for Money

In terms of value for money, proposal 2 is probably more likely to achieve this objective as it has the highest rankings on all the activity measures.

Objective 3 – Improving Health

This objective will be largely unaffected by the choice of proposal, although if proposals 1 and 2 allow recruitment of higher calibre staff and better retention of existing staff there could be a positive impact on the development and implementation of public health policies.

Objective 4 – Stakeholder interests

The proposal that assists the most with the achievement of objective 4 is more difficult to assess. To some extent it depends on the stakeholder being considered. Each group is discussed, briefly, below.

Patients will probably benefit most from proposal 2 in clinical terms, although many may prefer proposal 1 (or even proposal 3) because of greater convenience of location.

Staff may benefit most from proposal 1 as there is no indication this proposal will have any negative effects. The impact of proposal 2 on staff currently working in the services to be demerged has not been fully considered. Those in maternity and child welfare may benefit because of the scope for greater specialisation. The impact of private sector management on mental health services is impossible to judge, but experience from hospitals in other regions which have taken similar decisions has not been universally positive.

The government and local politicians will no doubt prefer the proposal that gives the greatest improvement in activity measures, which is proposal 2. However, they will also want the proposal that causes least complaint and unrest, which is proposal 1, or even proposal 3. This is a difficult trade off for this group of stakeholders.

Suppliers is the one group of stakeholders that may prefer proposal 3 outright. MGH sources its consumable supplies locally. If ArkFin acquires the contract to supply ancillary services then these local companies will lose substantial amounts of business and some smaller ones may have to close, with resultant loss of jobs in the community.

It is fair to say that prioritising the variables is a difficult task, especially those that are qualitative rather than quantitative. To aid the decision we extended the ranking and weighting exercise to include the "contribution to objectives" issues discussed in this section. We have assumed equal weighting of objectives and allocated a score (rather than a rank) of between 1 and 3 (1 = very good, 2 = good, 3 = satisfactory) to each proposal depending on how it contributes to the achievement of the objective. To some extent the determination of these scores is subjective but they have been determined after much discussion among members of the project evaluation team and other staff.

		Proposal 1		*Proposal 2*		*Proposal 3*	
Objective	*Weight*	*Score*	*WS*	*Score*	*WS*	*Score*	*WS*
High Quality Health Care	0·25	1	0·25	1	0·25	3	0·75
Value for Money	0·25	3	0·75	1	0·25	2	0·50
Improving Health	0·25	2	0·50	1	0·25	3	0·75
Stakeholder Interests	0·25	1	0·25	2	0·50	3	0·75
Totals			1·75		1·25		2·75

On the basis of this evaluation, proposal 2 again becomes the most attractive choice.

5.0 RECOMMENDATIONS

In section 3 we identified eight strategic issues facing MGH at the present time. In section 4 we reviewed the strengths, weaknesses, threats and opportunities of each of the proposed redevelopment proposals. In this section we discuss recommendations of actions to address each issue, noting where relevant any concerns we have that need to be addressed before the recommendation could be implemented. All our recommendations are summarized as a list in Appendix E.

Each recommendation in the following section is referenced, for example R1, R2 etc. These reference numbers are used also in Appendix E for ease of cross-referencing.

5.1 Serious weaknesses in the management

This issue has been evident for some time. The recent board changes have done little more than provide a temporary solution. Our recommendations here are in two parts: immediate and longer term.

The immediate recommendation is that permanent appointments are made to the posts of Chair, Chief Executive and Director of Finance. Subsequently, an additional NED needs to be appointed, preferably from a clinical profession (R2).

Our second recommendation is that the Group's governance procedures be strengthened (R3). Responsibility for this should be placed in an appropriate department, such as Corporate Secretariat or HR.

5.2 Financial performance

Proposal 1 would contribute most to providing a surplus in the immediate future. However, we believe to choose this proposal for this reason would put short-term gain against longer term overall benefits.

Our main recommendation here (R4) is to undertake an immediate review of the deteriorating financial performance, in particular to:

- Try and ascertain why "other income" is declining;
- Review all costs to determine if there could be cost savings introduced without affecting service quality.

5.3 Government targets and performance measures

These are a given and must be achieved if MGH is not to lose funding and reputation. The adoption of either redevelopment proposal 1 or 2 will help MGH meet targets, and in many cases exceed the minimum expectations based on the averages of comparative organisations. The introduction of a balanced scorecard approach will also assist in monitoring performance in target areas.

Only proposal 2 exceeds the target efficiency gains percentage for rebuild projects (3·38% compared with target of 3%) although proposal 3 is very close to target (0·99% against a target for refurbishment projects of 1%). Proposal 1 falls short of the target (2·91% compared with 3%) ,In terms of meeting the efficiency adjusted cost savings percentage, all three proposals meet the minimum requirement, with proposal 2 exceeding it.

Our recommendation (R5) is to set improvement targets for the coming year, independently of the evaluation of the three proposals.

5.4 Poor, outdated buildings and facilities

This issue can only be addressed by implementing one of the redevelopment proposals. The advantages and disadvantages of each were discussed in section 4. On almost all criteria, proposal 2 was the preferred choice. It ranked most highly on most of the evaluation criteria although it does not meet the required return on investments when lease payments are taken into account. Recommendation 1.3 below addresses this issue.

Our main recommendation (R1) is that the MGH Board adopts proposal 2. The project evaluation team will then need to be converted to a Project Management Team. The members of that team may or may not be the same people as are currently on the project evaluation team but this is a management issue yet to be discussed.

We also recommend that the surplus land is retained by MGH for future likely development (R1.1). There is a "real option" feature here; given the changing demographic profile of the region, there may be future requirements for, say, elderly care facilities that could be built here. If the land is sold MGH could be back to the situation of split sites.

Our main concerns about adopting this recommendation are:

1. Planning permission for housing development on the old land and buildings is refused;
2. Public objection to the proposal causes serious delays and disruptions;
3. The lease terms contain a risk, as discussed in section 4.

The first two concerns need active management and, if our main recommendation is adopted, we make three further recommendations:

- Establish a project management team (R1.2);

- MGH appoints a representative to the project management team to initiate discussion with ArkFin about the terms of the lease (R1.3). One possibility is that the length of the lease is extended to 30 or more years. This is not untypical of redevelopment projects of this type. As part of these negotiations, we could enquire if they would be interested in buying the old land and buildings as part of the overall financing arrangements. This would not be uncommon in deals of this kind and would have two advantages: ease of sale of the old land and buildings and possible favourable impact on terms of financing. The main disadvantage is the potential opportunity costs of profit foregone if the land and buildings could be sold for a higher sum on the open market. The fact that an independent valuer has valued the land provids some measure of confidence here.

The third concern is more problematic. We cannot, of course, prove that ArkFin is dangerously under pricing its 25 year lease terms, but we suggest the issue is included in the discussions with ArkFin about the purchase of the old land and buildings.

5.5 Resource limitations: staff and money

To some extent, this is an issue that will never be fully resolved for the reasons explained in section 3. Where demand exceeds supply, services are free at the point of delivery and public expectations constantly increase there will always be resource pressures. Our recommendation to adopt redevelopment proposal 2, which is the proposal with the highest NPV, will provide the greatest value for money and the most improvements in service delivery, but is not the cheapest proposal in terms of capital and financing costs.

When lease costs are taken into account, all three proposals show negative NPVs, with Proposal 3 being the least negative. However, as noted earlier, taking lease payments based on commercial rates of interest may not be appropriate for the investment decision here.

On a comparison between ArkFin and the International Bank, ArkFin should be allowed to provide finance for the contract. It is considerably cheaper than the competitive bidder. However, the concerns expressed earlier in this report should be considered.

Proposal 2 is likely to be popular with most staff, which should aid retention of personnel. The introduction of a balanced scorecard approach recommended above will also contribute to the organisation's ability to measure and monitor what is most important to MGH in terms of its objectives and strategic aims.

There are two specific recommendations:

- Improve staff relations and retentions in the immediate future by better communications. The HR department could be made responsible for establishing policy and procedures here (R7);

- Launch a recruitment campaign for key staff by emphasising the advantages of the Mayah region and the potential offered by the new facilities. Recruitment could be extended overseas subject to controls on language ability and equivalence of qualifications (R8).

5.6 Marketing/PR issues

This is an issue that needs urgent attention if other strategic issues are to be addressed. In particular, staff need to be retained and the public won over to the redevelopment proposal choice.

The recommendation is to strengthen the marketing function and make it a main board responsibility (R9).

5.7 Balancing the needs of the various stakeholder groups

If our recommendation to adopt redevelopment proposal 2 is approved, this recommendation will help meet the needs of most of the stakeholder groups, with the possible exception of suppliers and some patient groups. The introduction of a balanced scorecard approach has been discussed as a way forward.

A NED, Carlos Cluntz, identified the need to translate strategic objectives into tangible goals and actions at a Board meeting last year and we recommend here that he is asked to Chair a Committee to review the development and implementation of the BSC framework (R6).

5.8 Demographic changes

The forecast changes in the demographic profile of the region have significant implications for MGH. The current evaluation of the redevelopment proposals was based on current forecasts. The need in 10 years time may now be for less maternity/child welfare and more geriatric and age-related treatments. The new forecast reinforces the decision to proceed with redevelopment proposal 2. The merging of maternity services and child welfare with another region makes even more sense if this is a diminishing market. Similarly, as noted above, the retention of the surplus land if proposal 2 is adopted allows flexibility of use for changing requirements.

Nevertheless, our final recommendation is that a full evaluation of the implications for MGH should be initiated as soon as possible (R10). This might involve collection of additional data and more robust statistical demographic trend forecasts for the region.

Appendix A

EFFECT OF REDEVELOPMENT PROPOSALS ON MGH'S SURPLUS/DEFICIT

Forecast of annual profit or loss:

	Proposal 1 €(m)	*Proposal 2* €(m)	*Proposal 3* €(m)
Income (table 1 un-seen)	266·250	246·000	253·310
Other income (note 1)	14·500	14·500	14·500
Current expenses	(257·350)	(257·350)	(257·350)
Profit impact of expense adjustments:			
For activity (note 2)	(8·750)	(4·053)	(2·702)
Staff cost savings (note 3)	+3·991	+9·803	nil
Efficiency savings	+7·760	+8·320	+2·510
Surplus/-deficit on activities before interest and lease costs	+26·401	+17·220	+10·268

Notes:

1. The latest figure for the current year has been used. This could be too conservative since this was €23·5 million last year, and MGH is in a relatively affluent area and with an increasing ageing population who may wish to pay privately. The decline could have been a blip.

2. Current year costs are €257·350 (appendix C in the pre-seen) of which 75% are fixed costs (appendix B in the pre-seen). Therefore current fixed costs are €257·350 x 75% = €193·013. The adjustment for activity related costs (Table 1 in the unseen) are then calculated as follows:

Proposal 1: €257·350 x 25% x 13·6% increase = €8·750

Proposal 2: This is more difficult to quantify and more assumptions are needed. Although table 1 (un-seen) shows a 21·4% increase in activity the income from activities at €246 million is only around 6·3% higher than the current year's income for MGH. Information in the pre-seen states that volumes will decrease for proposal 2 because of the loss of maternity and health care patients. Although different kinds of patients will be funded differently by the government, a practical solution would be to treat variable costs increasing by only 6·3% (in line with income) that is €257·350 x 25% x 6·3% = €4·053.

Proposal 3: €257·350 x 25% x 4·2% increase = €2·702

3. Staff costs are 75% of current costs. Under proposal 1 these will fall to 73% and under proposal 2 to 70%. These savings are therefore calculated as:

   Proposal 1 – (€257·350 + €8·750) x 75% x 2% = €3·991
   Proposal 2 – (€257·350 + 3·860) x 75% x 5% = €9·803
   Proposal 3 – no effect

Appendix B

INVESTMENT APPRAISAL OF REDEVELOPMENT PROPOSALS

Proposal 1

Year	*Cashflows €(m)*	*5% discount factor*	*Present value € (m)*	*Notes*
0	-25·0	1·000	-25·00	(1)
1-3	-145·0	0·908	-131·67	(2 & 3)
4	+30·0	0·823	+24·70	(4)
4-28	+11·751	12·175	+143·07	(5 & 6)
		Net present value over 28 years	+11·10	
4-28	-12·57	12·175	-153·04	(7)
		Net present value after lease costs	-141·95	

Notes:

1. Cost of Romstat land.
2. Building costs over 40 months (say 3 years).
3. Average discount factor for years 1 to 3.
4. Sale of current land and buildings.
5. Estimated savings for staff costs and efficiencies.
6. Cumulative discount factor for year 28 (14·898) less the cumulative discount factor for year 3 (2·723) that is 12·175 is for 25 years.
7. Lease costs including ancillary services, discounted at 5%.

Proposal 2

Year	*Cashflows €(m)*	*5% discount factor*	*Present value € (m)*	*Notes*
0	-25·0	1·000	-25·00	(1)
1-3	-115·0	0·908	-104·42	(2 & 3)
4	+24·0	0·823	+19·75	(4)
4-28	+18·12	12·175	+220·61	(5 & 6)
		Net present value over 28 years	+110·89	
4 – 28	-10·4	12·175	-126·89	(7)
		Net present value after lease costs	-15·68	

Notes:

1. Cost of Romstat land.
2. Building costs over 36 months.
3. Average discount factor for years 1 to 3.
4. Sale of current land and buildings. There could be further land sales of €8m in year 4 of the spare Romstat land.
5. Estimated savings for staffing costs and efficiencies.
6. Cumulative discount factor for year 28 (14·898) less the cumulative discount factor for year 3 (2·723) that is 12·175 is for 25 years.
7. Lease costs including ancillary services, discounted at 5%.

Proposal 3

Year	*Cashflows €(m)*	*5% discount factor*	*Present value € (m)*	*Notes*
1-3	-35·0	0·908	-31·78	(1 & 2)
4-28	+2·51	12·175	+30·56	(3 & 4)
Net present value over 28 years			-1·22	
4-18	-4·6	8·966	-41·24	(5)
Net present value after lease costs			-42·46	

Notes:

1. Building costs over 36 months.
2. Average discount factor for years 1 to 3.
3. Estimated savings for efficiencies.
4. Cumulative discount factor for year 28 (14·898) less the cumulative discount factor for year 3 (2·723) that is 12·175. Proposal 3 evaluation had also been taken over 25 operational years to be comparable with proposals 1 and 2.
5. Lease costs over 15 years, discounted at 5%.

Appendix C – BALANCED SCORECARD

Client Perspective
Aim:
To deliver high quality health care
Existing:
Outpatient waiting times
Inpatient waiting times

Proposed:
For example:

Reduction in mortality [from disease]
Elderly care
Accident and emergency
Time to be seen
Patient satisfaction

Internal Process Perspective
Aim:
Improving Health
Existing:
none given

Proposed:
For example:

Reduction smoking related diseases
Reduction obesity

Learning and Growth Perspective
Aim:
Stakeholder interests
Existing:
None noted

Proposed:
For example:
Staff satisfaction levels
Reduction staff turnover

Cost Perspective
Aim:
Value for money
Existing:
Spending within limits
Staff costs as percentage
Av costs

Proposed:
For example:
Reduction management costs

Appendix D

Performance measures

	Current			% improvement on			% improvement on			% improvement on	
	Mayah	*Comparative Orgs*	*Proposal 1*	*Current*	*Comparative Orgs*	*Proposal 2*	*Current*	*Comparative Orgs*	*Proposal 3*	*Current*	*Comparative Orgs*
Hospital waiting times											
Out-patients:											
Within 3 months	0·68	0·60	0·75	10·29	25·00	0·80	17·65	33·33	0·72	5·88	20·00
In-patients:											
Within 3 months	0·65	0·75	0·78	20·00	4·00	0·80	23·08	6·67	0·70	7·69	-6·67
Within 12 months	0·95	1	1	5·26	0·00	1	5·26	0·00	1	5·26	0·00
Complaints											
Number	1,250	950	1,050	16·00	-10·53	950	24·00	0·00	1,150	8·00	-21·05
Upheld	175	50	75	57.14	-50·00	60	65·71	-20·00	80	54·29	-60·00
Staff complaints	185	85	85	54·05	0·00	50	72·97	41·18	65	64·86	23·53
Financial											
Under/over spend	-0·05	0	0			0			0		
Staff costs as % of total operating costs	0·75	0·7	0·73	2·67	-4·29	0·7	6·67	0·00	0·75	0·00	-7·14
Average cost per out-patient €	850	775	775	8·82	0·00	765	10·00	1·29	825	2·94	-6·45
Average cost per in-patient €	1,450	1,425	1,550	-6·90	-8·77	1,425	1·72	0·00	1,550	-6·90	-8·77

Appendix E – SUMMARY OF RECOMMENDATIONS

1 Adopt redevelopment proposal 2:

   1.1 Retain surplus land under proposal 2;

   1.2 Establish a project management team;

   1.3 Appoint representative to PMT to manage the concerns about the terms of the lease, including discussions with ArkFin on purchase of old land and buildings.

2 Make permanent appointments to the senior board positions currently held by temporary or acting staff and the NED vacancy.

3 Establish formal responsibility for corporate governance in an appropriate department.

4 Review deteriorating financial performance, especially "other income" and potential for cost savings.

5 Set targets independent of the proposals being evaluated.

6 Establish a committee to evaluate the adoption of a balanced scorecard approach to performance management under the chairmanship of Carlos Cluntz.

7 Allocate responsibility for staff communications to the HR department.

8 Launch a national and international recruitment campaign.

9 Strengthen the marketing/PR function and make it a main board responsibility.

10 Initiate a review of the implications for MGH of the forecast change in demographic profile of the region.

Order Form

For CIMA Official Study Materials for 2005 Exams

Qty	Title	Authors	ISBN	Price	Total
	CIMA Official *Study Systems*		**Available Now**		
	Performance Evaluation	Scarlett	0750664088	£33.00	
	Decision Management	Wilks	0750664096	£33.00	
	Risk and Control Strategy	Collier / Agyei-Ampomah	075066410X	£33.00	
	Financial Accounting and Tax Principles	Rolfe	0750664118	£33.00	
	Financial Analysis	Gowthorpe	0750664126	£33.00	
	Financial Strategy	Ogilvie	0750664134	£33.00	
	Organisational Management and Information Strategy	Perry	0750664142	£33.00	
	Integrated Management	Harris / Sims	0750664150	£33.00	
	Business Strategy	Botten / Sims	0750664169	£33.00	
	TOPCIMA	Sims / Barnwell	0750664177	£33.00	
	CIMA Official *Revision Cards*				
	Performance Evaluation	Scarlett	0750664819	£6.95	
	Decision Management	Avis	0750664827	£6.95	
	Risk and Control Strategy	Harris	0750664835	£6.95	
	Financial Accounting and Tax Principles	Rolfe	0750664878	£6.95	
	Financial Analysis	Gowthorpe	0750664886	£6.95	
	Financial Strategy	Ogilvie	0750664894	£6.95	
	Organisational Management and Information Systems	Perry	0750664843	£6.95	
	Integrated Management	Harris	0750664851	£6.95	
	Business Strategy	Botten	075066486X	£6.95	
	CIMA Official *Exam Practice Kits*				
	Performance Evaluation	Barnett / Dawkins	0750665882	£14.95	
	Decision Management	Barnett / Dawkins	0750665890	£14.95	
	Risk and Control Strategy	Robertson	0750665920	£14.95	
	Financial Accounting and Tax Principles	Patel / Channer	0750665904	£14.95	
	Financial Analysis	Rodgers	0750665912	£14.95	
	Financial Strategy	Graham	0750665939	£14.95	
	Organisational Management and Information Systems	Robertson	0750665874	£14.95	
	Integrated Management	Best / Dalton	0750665815	£14.95	
	Business Strategy	Graham	0750665823	£14.95	
	TOPCIMA	Little	0750666277	£14.95	
	CIMA CPD *Introduction to Business Tax*	Jones	0750666390	£44.99	
		Postage and packing		£2.95	
		TOTAL			

Elsevier retains certain personal information about you in hard copy form and on computer. It will be used to inform you about goods and services from Elsevier and its associated companies in which you may be interested. ☐ Please tick this box if you do not want to receive this information.

ELSEVIER

CIMA PUBLISHING

Post this form to:

CIMA Publishing Customer Services
Elsevier
FREEPOST (OF 1639)
Linacre House, Jordan Hill
OXFORD, OX2 8DP, UK

Or **FAX** +44 (0)1865 474 010
Or **PHONE** +44 (0)1865 474 014
Email: cimaorders@elsevier.com
www.cimapublishing.com

Name: ____________

Organisation: ____________

Invoice Address: ____________

____

____

____

Postcode: ____________

Phone number: ____________

Email: ____________

Delivery Address if different:

FAO ____________

Address ____________

____

____

____

Postcode ____________

Please note that all deliveries must be signed for

1. Cheques payable to Elsevier.

2. Please charge my:

☐ Visa/Barclaycard ☐ Access/Mastercard
☐ American Express ☐ Diners Card
☐ Switch Issue No.______

Card No. ____________

Expiry Date ____________

Cardholder Name: ____________

Signature: ____________

Date: ____________